ALSO AVAILABLE BY

Stephen Rich Merriman

Behavioral Addictions:
A New Solution to Very Old Problems

Anger and Rage Addiction & The Self-Pact:
New Lights on an Old Nemesis

Pathfinding Through Multiple Personality

The Living Oracle:
Wisdom & Divination for Everyday Life

Outside Time: My Friendship with Wilbur

Who's at Home in Your Body (When You're Not)?

When You Lose What You Can't Live Without

(ed.) *Speak But the Word:*
From Multiple Personalities to Wholeness

the subtler points I was endeavoring to capture, and convey, in language. I am grateful to him for his help during both phases—the stubborn denial of "*not* wanting to," and the capitulation to the reality that "I guess I'm really doing this."

My other, and *foremost*, Thank You!! is to my beloved wife and soulmate Emily Sara Taylor Merriman, who, from the very beginning (with many years of practice under her belt in "knowing me"), knew *exactly* what I was up to, even before I did. Emily's love and support, along with her discerning professional eye in the entwined areas of both writing *and* content, have been a steady and stabilizing presence during the writing of this book, and a helpful supportive influence on me personally—both crucial factors in this book's coming to be. On those occasions in which I would start to doubt the worth of what I was writing, she would embolden me, in her loving, quiet, way, to continue on with it. When I would pull out of the "mini-doldrums" and feel better about how things were going, she was right there with me, with loving nudges and enthusiastic support. Emily also created this beautiful work of art that graces the front and back covers of this book. What a wonderful invocation it is! She has taught me, both in marriage and in critiquing my writing, what that venerable old quality of "constancy" really means—what it truly is to "have someone's back." My gratitude for her love, her help, and for who she is, knows no limits.

I also wish to express my appreciation to James McDonald, a most masterful book designer, who took on the stout challenge of turning my highly idiosyncratic text into a beautifully crafted book—to my eye a most splendid and devotion-laden work of art. As the final book was taking shape, we have had a wonderfully collaborative relationship, along with a likely friendship to follow. Thank you James.

How fortunate I am to have such a crucible of loving, sustained support. My good fortune is not lost on me. It's joyful to experience "happiness"—and to *know it*.

Foreword

The Self-Pact: Harnessing "Triggering," Exploring Self-Discovery, Attaining Personal Liberation, is, in large part, a book about "Triggering," a phenomenon that is so pervasive and, on (or off) balance, profoundly misgauged as to its provenance, dynamics, and life-destroying implications.

For those of us who are "Triggerers," and have found ourselves in lots of hot water resulting from our own triggering and subsequent unleashings, a way, perhaps a method, certainly a "path," came into being about 12 years ago. This path has proven capable of ameliorating damage previously inflicted by our triggering nature on our loved ones—spouses, children, and friends —through a method that actually is capable of harnessing these heretofore destructive Energies unleashed by triggering. These Energies, it was discovered, could be "held," in full potency, "harnessed," and "ridden inwards"—rather than unleashed "outwards." They have also proven capable of leading us into inner encounters that have been able to reveal to us our early life circumstances—the "original causes and conditions" which, unbeknownst to us, have formed, and dis-formed, us into who we thought, and were convinced, we were.

The means for launching, and accomplishing, all this is called *The Self-Pact*. This book builds upon nearly 12 years of experience with the Self-Pact since its inauguration in early July, 2009. The Self-Pact is a highly valuable technique, *and* process, in coming to terms with, and dealing with, the destructive ramifications of triggering—including, not just the emotional mayhem of anger and rage, but, additionally, the destructiveness of a whole panorama of powerful emotions which are also prone, for those of us with traumatic, or conflict-based backgrounds, to being triggered—to disruptive and damaging effect, capable of destroying lives.

A note on the words "triggerers," "triggerings," "energy" (and "energies") and their numerous variants: These words show up very frequently in this text.

The Self-Pact:

Harnessing "Triggering,"
Exploring Self-Discovery,
Attaining Personal Liberation

The Self-Pact:

Harnessing "Triggering,"
Exploring Self-Discovery,
Attaining Personal Liberation

Stephen Rich Merriman, Ph.D.

Four Rivers Press

Amherst, Massachusetts

FOURRIVERSPRESS.COM

Cover painting by Emily Sara Taylor Merriman

Book design by James McDonald
JAMESMCDONALDBOOKS.COM

ISBN: 978-0-9817698-8-2

LIBRARY OF CONGRESS CONTROL NUMBER
2021906512
LIBRARY OF CONGRESS SUBJECT HEADINGS
Self-Acceptance
Self-Realization
Adjustment (Psychology)
Change (Psychology)

PRINTED IN VARIOUS LOCATIONS WORLDWIDE

The Self-Pact: Harnessing *"Triggering,"*
Exploring Self-Discovery, Attaining Personal Liberation
is dedicated to all those who find the courage,
born of necessity, to face their own darkness,
and, in following that darkness into the light,
become who they are meant to be.

Contents

Acknowledgements

IT'S ALWAYS A WONDERFUL EVENT to be far enough along with authoring a book that it becomes time to thank, both in general and specific ways, the people, the forces, and, yes, the workings of divine Providence, that can, collectively, get a "book" brewing in the *unconscious mind*, even while the "person," whose "mind" it (supposedly) is, doesn't have a clue that this is happening. Ego consciousness is oftentimes, during this period of early fertility that is unfolding beneath the realm of conscious intention, dead set against "ever again writing another damn book!!"

That about describes the process that stirred up the latent soup on this one. I am grateful to have a very determined "unconsciousness" (unconscious *only* to me, **not** to itself!) that refused to let "conscious intention"—nominally, "me"— squash *its* own expressive needs out of being realized.

The truth is that—notwithstanding the considerable experience I have had with the Self-Pact, and the absolute trust I've found to be well placed in it as it has assisted me with issues of grave consequence which, if left unattended, threatened to destroy me—I was *not* eager to author this book because of the emotional taxation writing about this material exacts from me. In other words, I was not at all eager to "put myself through it." So now . . . having gotten this far, I recognize and celebrate my own unconscious process for persisting to the point that I awakened to *its* intentions, and accepted the role I was to play in helping to make them manifest.

Because this whole process of creating this book has been *SO* interior, the individuals who have been aware that I was "up to something" (without my being more specific about what it was I was actually writing) are relatively few in number. These included my grown children Hannah, Hardy and Joely, and my nine-year old child E. To E. I want to express my special thanks for sharing, while involved in on-line activities, the living room couch with me. As I was working hard, at the other end of the sofa, both transcribing the original longhand text into printed text, and then, subsequently, editing the book, every once in a while two feet would suddenly appear from under E.'s blanket and nudge me in the leg. I would gently re-cover the tootsies, folding the blanket back over them. This happened on many occasions, especially when the house was cold. (It was winter, after all.) That diffused kind of togetherness was a soul tonic for us both. Collectively, my children did not really know *what* I was up to, but they were relieved that I was not playing, during this pandemic, "couch potato." At least, as they saw it, I was *"up to something!"*

I also wish to acknowledge our two cats, Jasper and Goldie, for teaching me a great deal about the phenomenon of triggering. Watching then has taught me why it is that you can't "herd cats." The reason you can't? They live in a near-constant state of triggering and triggerability. This, apparently, is true of all felines. They are constantly on "red alert," and live out their lives that way. Jasper and Goldie will never know how they have taught me, but I can, and do, express my love and appreciation to them by plying them with spontaneous purr-producing abundances of gentle, non-triggering pats.

Among the individuals who DID know what I was up to, there are two: I wish to acknowledge the persistent steadfastness and gentle encouragement of Dr. Eugene Goldwater, a psycho-analyst by training, who (rare for that profession) also became, over the course of his career, a proficient expert in the realm of addictions diagnosis and treatment. This is an unusual combination of expertise. Dr. Goldwater was my sounding board as I, initially, was very expressive of my reluctance to "start another book." After crossing the divide into actually commencing to write, as my focus was increasingly sharpened by the very content I was writing, we had numerous fine discussions as to some of

"Triggerers" ("Trigger," "Triggering," "Triggerings" and the like), from this point forward in this book, are almost always expressed with the capital "T" prefix. This is to distinguish between the instinctual "triggering" inheritance we all are born with, stemming from "fight, flight and freeze" reactions—the neurology of which having accrued over countless generations from our primordial, prehistoric origins—and the Triggerings of personal experience (hence, within a given lifetime) which, while building on the original inheritance of instinct, go further in specifying Triggerings *that are emotional links, and, rather than life preserving, usually spill in the direction of life-destroying*.

Regarding the words "energy" (and "energies"), they are spelled-out—presented—in a number of different ways, depending on the particular emphasis that is being expressed by the author (while in the process of writing each individual passage). So . . . you will see a range of variations of that simple word "energy" such as "energy," "Energy," "ENERGY," "ENERGY!!," *THE ENERGY!!!* (along with equivalent variants for the plural form "energies"). Again, *these variations speak to the range of intensities intended to be communicated by the author*—intensities, moment by moment, he was experiencing as he wrote the material in this book. They can be thought of as a visual equivalent of the English grammatical construction called "onomatopœia." However, unlike onomatopœia, in which "the sound suits the sense," here, the "visual onomatopœia" of the basic word, "energy" (or "energies"), "suits" or, rather, *depicts,* the intended intensity of the Energy under discussion.[1]

This exercise of "visual onomatopœia" also appears, from time to time, with the word "emotion." For example, along with other uses, you will occasionally encounter a formula featuring "E-Motion." It goes like this:

E-Motion = Energy-In-Motion.

---

1. Of course, in making the case for minting "visual onomatopœia," I'm aware that, in doing so, I've resorted to an example of alliteration. The example I chose meets both the criteria of alliteration and onomatopœia.

(I won't comment on this formula further at this point, except to say that, as you read this book, it's a good one to bear in mind.)

As a closing note in this topic, I would simply mention that, much later in the book, the terms "resonance"and "shrapnel" receive expressive treatment similar to "energy"and "emotion." (Somewhat sheepishly, I confess that, for better or worse, rather than conform to cultural expectations of correct linguistic propriety, I come down on the side of bending language to serve my expressive needs, rather than contorting myself to meet conventional expectations as to "proper usage"—at the expense of losing some aspect of what needs to be conveyed.)

Finally, I want you to know that this book is written in the form of a monograph. The monograph itself is about 130 pages from start to finish. There are numerous sections to the monograph, and these sections are labeled. They denote various topic changes (as well as certain repetitions) and other shared information, as needed. They are not, however, discrete "chapter headings." The book is simply a monograph, start to finish.

Well, that's about it. I'm eager enough to have you wade into this book that I'm going to keep the "Foreword" short. I've held you up long enough from what awaits you!

I end, for now, with a kind of invocation:

May *The Self-Pact: Harnessing "Triggering," Exploring Self-Discovery, Attaining Personal Liberation* be a source, and a means, for you, my beloved readers, should your life circumstances hold you in serious need of it, to attain constructive, loving and healing resolution to the quandary of being a Triggerer. May this book be of true value, and real assistance to you as you continue on the path of becoming—*not* necessarily the person you feel you *have* to be, nor the one you feel you *should* be, but, rather ... the person, within your "life purpose," you are *meant* to be.

—Stephen Rich Merriman
March 24th, 2021
Pioneer Valley, Western Massachusetts

The Self-Pact: Harnessing "Triggering," Exploring Self-Discovery, Attaining Personal Liberation

Introduction: BIG "First Steps," The path to the Self-Pact

My Dear Readers,

It is a privilege to bring you up-to-date on the use of the Self-Pact, first as a way to stop wounding people when Triggered, and second, in so doing, discovering the Self-Pact to be an unanticipated vehicle for personal growth, liberation and freedom.

As I commence this writing, it's coming up on eleven and a half years (first week of July, 2009) since an insight, amidst considerable personal suffering, burst upon me, ultimately setting me forth in a direction I could not have anticipated.

At that time, I had already amassed, one day at a time, long-term recovery from active alcoholism (38 years sober as of then), and had come to recognize that the energy underlying active alcoholism and drug addiction was the same energy—an *Energy!*—that had fueled, *and was continuing to fuel,* various behaviors in the non-alcoholism/non-drug-addiction sphere.

The challenge that I had to deal with, as of early July, 2009, was anger and rage addiction. Many years previous (mid-1970s), when I was sober for about five and a half years from active alcoholism, I had faced, in its extremeness, a similar challenge with sex and 'love' addiction. At that time I endured a brutal, but sustained, withdrawal from that form of "acting out." I had come to terms with it, and, since that time, had (and have) lived my way into long-term recovery from it.

I HAD HELD ON TO HIGH HOPES that with these major hurdles of moving decisively away from the two such destructive addictions (active alcoholism and sex and 'love' addiction) now behind me, consistent, sustained and constant vigilance, one day at a time, might lead me onwards to an enlightened plateau of healing, in which I would find myself relieved of the burden of living under the duress of obsession and compulsion; they would no longer be in my mix. It was a worthy wish, and I sincerely believed I deserved it (!) . . . but, a bigger picture needed to reveal itself that might offer me a more encompassing understanding of my plight, and the depths it would be necessary to, electively, descend to, in order to be able to touch base with the fundaments—the original causes and conditions—of my being.

Unbeknownst to me, that episode in early July, 2009 is when anger and rage, and the insights that burst forth from them, were to offer me a path downwards into the miasma of "original causes and conditions," the outflow from which having possessed me and, again unbeknownst to me, driven me in destructive, self-defeating fashion over many decades.

Discovering, and following, that path was, in the fullness of time, made possible by a sacred commitment to a new relationship with myself called the Self-Pact. And . . . the Self-Pact could *only* be minted by extreme suffering of my own making. In my case it arose, not through active alcoholism (despite some raw suffering there), nor from sex and 'love' addiction (tremendous amount of suffering and destruction there). It arose in what I came to recognize, and call, anger and rage addiction, the full awareness and negative impact of which (as I have mentioned) arising many years later into "recovery."

The Self-Pact became viable to me because, having already

gone to considerable lengths (using traditional behavioral modification strategies—all unsuccessful) to tame my "anger and rage unleashing" problem, it was the only option left that was available to me—and the discovery that such an option might even exist was in itself the minting of new awareness. Inaugerating and following the Self-Pact, my destructive behavior, involving the unleashing of rage and anger on the outer world and creating victims there, was profoundly curtailed. My marriage (with the woman who is the love of my life) was saved, and the depths of what needed to unfold and be recognized within me became *accessible.* The lessening of victimizing targets in the outer world, in conjunction with a vast inner terrain of psychical activity (the former paving the way for the latter to open to being acknowledged and explored) carried me along for several years. New discoveries and deeper probings of self became living realities for me. My creativity and resourcefulness were once again blooming as I shared news about the Self-Pact and what it was producing in me with a few trusted friends and colleagues, who (less desperate than I was and as more of an experiment) inaugurated their own Self-Pact journeys—with some reporting significant results.

At the four-year point following the inception of the Self-Pact, enough time had elapsed, enough experiences aggregated, and enough people having tried it with relevant results, that I felt the time was right to write a book about it—with the Self-Pact, at that time, specifically geared only to anger and rage addiction. It seemed time to make the availability of this new technique accessible to all those who could benefit from it.

Hence, my book *Anger and Rage Addiction & The Self-Pact: New Lights on an Old Nemesis* was published (Four Rivers Press, 2013[1]). The "good news!" was now out there to be shared with, and drawn upon by, anyone who could use it.

It is my intention here to re-present, in a more abbreviated

---

1. Available via fourriverspress.com

way, the whole structure and implementation of the Self-Pact. That whole process was originally set forth in all its painstaking detail in *Anger and Rage Addiction & the Self-Pact*. At the time that book was written, the excitement of the Self-Pact dynamics was still intense (arguably, the language in that ground-breaking book may strike the reader as being a "bit over-the-top"—reflective of the enthusiasm stemming from some early discoveries arising from using the Self-Pact, rather than being merely just some verve-driven promotional hustle).

What I *will* do here is outline a few principles of the Self-Pact that will enable the reader to move forward with me as I subsequently share deeper material in this book, stemming from a much larger and longer involvement with the Self-Pact. This presentation of preliminary principles of the Self-Pact should not be regarded—*especially by those of my readers who suspect they have* destructive *"anger and rage" dynamics happening in their lives*—as a substitute for reading the earlier book. It is in *that* book that both the principles, techniques, and numerous additional salient points are presented in necessary detail for those who may feel motivated to try the Self-Pact on for size. Those who are prone to Triggering in areas that are *not* as explosive as anger and rage may find sufficient information and shared experience in this book to launch their own adventures, however even in less serious circumstances the original book still holds a greater amount of detail regarding the specifics of launching the Self-Pact, and what to expect from it.

So, let's begin. Here are a handful of preliminary details regarding what the Self-Pact consists of:

THE SELF-PACT IS A DEAL one makes with oneself—between "me" and "me."

[A **note** about "me" and "me" ("you" and "you")]:
The Self-Pact is a pact between "you" and "yourself"—"between "you" and "you." In phrasing the participants in this way, the Self-Pact acknowledges a reality of the human condition. It is this:

Insofar as our neurology is constantly rearranging in accordance with our experience of our "moods" (each mood, having, within us, its own discrete neurological arrangement), we, each one of us, are, at some level, a pluralistic entity. For instance, the "rageful I" has a very different level of neurological (along with endocrinal/hormonal) engagement than the subsequent contrite, guilt-ridden, remorseful "me." The body our words and emotions express through may be singular, but there are very many discrete neurological/glandular/hormonal presences that make themselves felt within each, and every, human body.

So, in addressing and forging a Self-Pact between "me" and "me," the Self-Pact is a trans-ego(s), or trans-mood(s) agreement. It is knowingly entered into not solely by me—the presiding ego-presence of the moment—but by those components of my being (which does, indeed, include "me" and my neurological constellation), *along with them and their respective neurologies that are operative in, collectively, our emotions-infused realities.*

In other words, the Self-Pact is established between "me," and all concerned inner arrangements—neurological and hormonal— of "me."

Here is a brief précis of what the Self-Pact consists of— again, in outline form—not necessarily enough for you to dive in and use it, but likely enough for you to "get the hang" of what it's all about.

The Four Declarations of the Self-Pact

The *First Declaration* of the Self-Pact starts with the recognition, admission, acceptance and declaration to oneself that:

(1) "I am a person who Triggers, and there is nothing I can do to keep myself from Triggering—to keep Triggering from happening."

NOTE: This means that Triggering is accepted as an *unavoidable* reality in our lives—all the more so for those of us who have experienced (were subjected to) traumatic occurrences in infancy, toddlerhood and subsequent childhood. For better or worse (richer or poorer, 'til death do us part), it's "baked in the cake"— an immovable reality which can't be begged, borrowed, cajoled or otherwise persuaded to "take a hike," or "leave well enough alone." It's just there—a structural given.

This rueful reality means that—using anger and rage Triggering as an example—a person who rages (or who Triggers in any of the many other emotional fracture zones that exist within each of us) is not in control, either of shaping the expression of emotional energy, or shaping the expression of personal behavior. This outworking (again in terms of our anger and rage example) of what, in a child, would be termed a temper tantrum, *is brought on by a Triggering phenomenology that is fully launched in less than one-seventh (1/7th) the time it takes for rational faculties to be deployed to head it off.*

In other words, for someone who Triggers into anger and rage—and by inference for anyone who Triggers along any of their own emotional fracture zones—that person lives at the mercy of their Triggering neurology. In our example in the arena of anger and rage, for instance, the neurology of Triggering picks a person's fights for them, and reason "plays catch-up"—if even a smidgen of any "present-moment" attempt to moderate is to be applied to it. When neurological Triggering (in *any* area of experience) detonates, the limbic system's surge bypasses the frontal lobe—momentarily short-circuiting the seat of rational, conscious thinking. It takes 70 milliseconds (70 ms or 1/14th of a second) to Trigger, and by the time "reason" knows that this is happening . . . it's already happened. It's old news. Triggering already occurred four-hundred thirty milliseconds (430 ms— nearly half a second) earlier.[2] In summary, *it is structurally*

---

2. Neurological/synaptic network response source for this data: https://plato. stanford.edu/entries/consciousness-temporal/empirical-findings.html

impossible for rational consciousness to "get out ahead of" the phenomenon of Triggering.

The *Second Declaration* of the Self-Pact (and the Declarations that follow) move into the Pact commitments proper:

(2) "I make a pact that whenever (not if) I Trigger, I will acknowledge and accept the Energy of Triggering—the Energy!—as being present in me. I agree to accept the presence of the Energy."

NOTE: This component of the Self-Pact is an agreement between "me" and "me" (the foundation for which has already been addressed) *to acknowledge and accept the presence of Triggering as a predictable, and therefore expected, presence. The full presence of the Energy is acknowledged and, after a fashion, welcomed.*

The *Third Declaration* of the Self-Pact is:

(3) "When (not if) Triggered, I/we agree that I/we will go to any lengths to spare the outer world: the creation of any further victims, and any further victimization of past victims of my/our Triggering (Emotional unleashings)."

NOTE: The pact to go to any lengths to not create any further victims during the process of being Triggered is a sacred commitment. This aspect of the Self-Pact is NOT an attempt to in any way squelch or suppress the Energy of one's Triggered torments. *The Energy is fully present, and welcomed to be so.* In "sparing the outer world the creation of any additional victims," and foregoing "any further victimization of past victims," of whatever torments are Triggering, *the Energy is held, in full potency, while others are spared.* This is true regardless of any perceived provocations (either actual or imagined—when Triggered you can't tell them apart) from the outer world that may be claimed as having created or led to the Triggering event.

The *Fourth Declaration* of the Self-Pact is:

(4) "In full acknowledgment of the Third Declaration (above), I/we agree, when Triggered, to 'ride the Energy' of my/our Triggered torments: to let this Energy show me what it wants me to know, whatever kinds of experiences it wants me to have with it, whatever emotions and feelings it wants me to encounter, along with any awarenesses it wants to arise in me—by opening myself to let this Energy drive itself, along with my full awareness and participation, INWARDS."

NOTE: With the resolution, as a component of the Self-Pact, to "spare the world of causing additional victims," and foregoing "any further victimizations of past victims," even while acknowledging and accepting the presence of the Energy and its emotional torment—*that* Energy! now has only one direction where it can move—and that is INWARDS. "Riding the Energy inwards " is letting it, and "us," be harnessed to one another on an inward, mutual excursion.

These four *Declarations*:

(1) I am a person who Triggers, and there is nothing I can do to keep it from happening.

(2) Whenever I Trigger I will acknowledge and accept that the Energy of Triggering is present in me; I agree to accept the presence of this Energy, holding it in full potency rather than attempting to be rid of it.

(3) When Triggered I/we agree to go to any lengths to spare the outer world the creation of any new victims, and also spare the outer world any further victimization of past victims.

(4) When Triggered, I/we commit to riding the Energy of my/our Triggered torments *inwards*. I/we agree to let the Energy of Triggered torments show me what it wants me to know, including whatever kinds of experiences, feelings, emotions, awarenesses, memories it wants me to have, along with my full

awareness and presence—taking me wherever it wants to take me *INWARDS*—on the inside.

Collectively, these Four Declarations, between "me" and "me," *are* the Self-Pact.

NOTE: Regarding the sacredness of the Self-Pact: The Self-Pact is personal, sacred, and held as such. Establishing it "between 'me' and 'me'" is a sacred act. If a person who is afflicted with/by Triggering-caused torments is desperate enough to give themselves over fully to trying it, the sacredness of such an experience becomes a *"felt"* experience—no maudlin sentiments here—just a centered focus of attention and commitment combined with utter determination, taking on, in the aggregate, an unmistakable, integrated emotional hue.

More about the Self-Pact: challenges and early discoveries

IT IS NOT SURPRISING that the Self-Pact emerged out of the rough and tumble of Triggered anger and rage unleashings. Such unleashings are spectacular, high volume and (always) destructive occurrences. Therefore, as "Triggering events" which lead to the recognition of the dynamics of addiction that propelled them, they (anger and rage) were the first to be noted. In their severity, they required, in a sense, an equally severe, unrelenting offset that would, through its own intensity and correspondences, be capable of harnessing Triggered energy in furtherance of the cessation of destructive actions, and . . . becoming open to discovering a new level of self-knowledge and healing.

Once again, I utterly recommend that you read my earlier book *Anger and Rage Addiction and the Self- Pact: New Lights on an Old Nemesis,* to gain a further orientation regarding the applied dynamics of the Self-Pact with regards to its formative years as a "treatment" for anger and rage addiction. This will help prepare you for the increasing capabilities of the Self-Pact to be harnessed regarding a much wider range of Triggered phenomena than was in any way obvious during those first formative years of use. All that follows in this book is built on the foundation of those earlier years.

I'll mention in passing (**Not** a complete substitute for actually immersing yourself in the earlier book) a few of the awarenesses and awakenings that emerged in those earlier four years or so.

The first is that in attempting to meet the challenge of consciously holding the Energy of anger and rage after Triggering has occurred, *it was (is) possible to hold it—the Energy!—in full potency, without unloading it on the outer world.* An immediate plus that was realized is that injurious behaviors, including emotional abuse, physical abuse, sexual abuse, passion-driven self-righteousness, and lust for vindictive triumph, did *not* have to be unleashed. All this could be "held," and not inflicted on third parties.

So ... the BIG first breakthrough of consequence from establishing the Self-Pact was the near-complete cessation of injuring those who were, and are, nearest and dearest to us. This immediate outcome, even when one's own credibility about their commitment to the Self-Pact (given one's personal history of destruction) had been completely wanting in the beginning, was a huge immediate benefit for all concerned parties, and ... it was launched in the absence of, as yet, any further insights or awarenesses that "riding the Energy of anger and rage inwards" might produce.

The next (second) realization that started to arise from the act of actually harnessing the Energy of anger and rage and "riding it inwards"—a crucial tenet of the Self-Pact—was that this was (is) actually possible to do!! Recall that *with* the creation of victims in the outer world (regardless of perceived external provocations) now, as a condition of the Self-Pact, ruled out, the only pathway for the Energy of anger and rage to follow was (is) INWARDS. Was "traveling there" even possible? YES.

And the fact of actually being able to ride the Energy of

Triggered torments inwards led quite quickly to a major break-through in understanding.

Again, this breakthrough was minted in the arena of Triggered anger and rage, and later would be found to be applicable in a wide range of Triggered phenomena—but I'm ahead of myself. That comes later.

Here is the breakthrough, presented in "anger and rage addiction" terms:

The Energy of anger and rage, especially in its manifestations of anger and rage addiction—having features of Triggering, obsession, compulsion, confabulation, and amnesia—is, along with its out-workings of "unleashing," *always destructive.* However . . . *when this Energy, via the Self-Pact, is harnessed in service of "riding inwards," it can, and does, take on an additional hue. It serves to lead the prevailing ego-consciousness of the person who has established the Self-Pact into a vast inner world in which the Energy of anger and rage (in this instance) is augmented by, and eventually becomes more and more of,* **a guiding energy** *that leads that person into the realm of "original causes and conditions." In other words, the hands-down destructive Energy of anger and rage becomes, by degrees, transmuted into a guiding, revealing, even teaching Energy.* Who would have guessed that?!

The transmuting of such destructive potential (which has certainly not ceased to exist) into a pedagogical role that is potentially very constructive and even healing, qualifies as a real "fake-out" surprise in starting to follow the Self-Pact. It is difficult to overstate the relevance of this discovery.

With that recognition, in which (again expressed in anger and rage addiction terms) such a destructive Energy, knowingly and cooperatively turned inwards (riding its own Energy inwards), can function as a guide—maybe even as a bit of a psychopomp—the inner adventure of self-knowing—self-revelating—has begun.

The earlier awarenesses that the Self-Pact, in conjunction with the Energy, start to serve up to our larger cognitive recognitions: chronological memories, flashes of certain past (deep past) occurrences—these are registered somewhat as a kind of "information format." At other times, Emotional Energy starts to be felt *independent of cognitive linkages* (re: "Why am I feeling like this?") and takes on its own prevalent hue.

Another early milestone (third awareness) awaits, and it is this: The melange of powerful <u>E</u>motions that are "in-<u>M</u>otion," as interspersed with fragmentary, incomplete memory shards— all of which, in swirling fashion, going beyond cerebral "sense making"—*is*, as an immediate, current occurrence within the Self-Pact, *an exact replication—somatic, emotional, psychical—of one, maybe **the, prevailing experience of childhood**.*

The Self-Pact, in harnessing the Energy for inward journeying, is *not*, solely, a regressive experience. *Rather, the constellation of childhood torments, transcending mere description, now move from "past" to "present" as a **progressive**, rather than regressive, occurrence.* A person who has entered into the Self-Pact is, throughout the inner journeying, still present in the body as an adult, conscious participant in, and during, the inner journey, but . . . side by side with his or her own adult consciousness arises a kaleidoscope of resonances, partial memories, here-and-now "presences," cognitive awarenesses, random flashbacks, nameless impressions, along with seemingly extraneous "why-am-I-seeing-hearing-thinking-feeling-remembering-recalling" incursions of immersive infor-mation that go far beyond what is currently known, and suggest (or are forebears of) lines of inquiry and revelation that are yet to be opened and explored—yet to be *re-experienced*.

With such a Self-Pact experience, one has started to touch base with "original causes and conditions" that, unrecognized and unknown to everyday wakeful consciousness, have been "ruling the roost" for many years—even decades.

Curiously, in the area of anger and rage addiction (from which, as I never seem to tire of mentioning, the Self-Pact sprang into realization), a further, yet still early discovery (fourth discovery) of the Self-Pact's inner-journeying awaits. It is this: When a person has Triggered into venomous anger and rage, has defaulted instantly into Self-Pact mode (one of the tenets of the Self-Pact), has held the Energy in full potency, ridden it inwards, had whatever feelings, emotions, encounters, cognitive awareness, chronological memories, impressions, and realizations—along with touching, however tangentially, some aspect of "original causes and conditions" that may await on any such journey, and, sensing the conclusion of such a journeying episode, now returns back into "everyday," fully present consciousness in "consensus reality"—*that person may discover that s/he is no longer feeling rageful or vindictive.* In some mysterious way the Energy of toxic anger and rage—the Energy!—has been, through some level of contact with "original causes and conditions," palliated.

This experience, however initially meager it may be, of returning Energy to its source—and, in so doing, no longer (in this example expressed in anger and rage addiction terms) feeling hatred and rage towards the person, place, thing, situation, or circumstances in the "present" that, prior to this, were taken to be the "true" cause of the episode of Triggering and unleashing of the Energy of anger and rage—reveals starkly the power of psychological projection to "create" an apparent "cause" for Triggering based on current circumstances, or events—which, to ego-consciousness, is taken to be ***the real cause*** of the Triggering and unleashing, *only to dissipate like a wisp of smoke when a deeper,* **actual provenance—the actual, more deep-seated cause—***has been encountered via the Self-Pact.* The Energy!!, ridden inwards, has commenced to reveal the *true* state of affairs.

The larger vista unfolds

Anger and Rage Addiction & The Self Pact: New Lights on an Old Nemesis was written at about the four-year point following the inception of the Self-Pact. It was published in 2013. In the four years that had elapsed since the Self-Pact's beginnings, a number of people had experimented with it. They were listed (along with my gratitude for their having "tried it on for size") in the Acknowledgements page of that book.

The brainstorm that had lead to the conception of the Self-Pact as "the last house on the block" was, for me, the last chance to salvage what, in my case, was the final opportunity to spare myself a pathetic, destructive, toxic legacy, complete with passing this "toxicity" along to my spouse and children (already born or yet to be). However, the desperation that had led in my case to the breakthrough was not the life circumstance for most of those who tried the Self-Pact on for size. Whereas, in addition to having a history of active alcoholism, sex addiction, 'love' addiction, and anger and rage addiction that was baked into my marrow—notwithstanding that I was, at the time of the Self-Pact launching, long sober from active alcoholism (38 years clean and sober as of that point), my active sex and 'love' addiction (33 years clean and sober as of that point), and anger and rage addiction (4 years into the Self-Pact with a growing marriage of increasing love, trust, intimacy and devotion rooted in a firm foundation), those who tried out the Self-Pact as curious participants did have a role, unclear at the time, in the evolution of what was to follow: *the expansion of awareness about the prevalence of Triggerable Emotions,* **NOT** *limited to anger and rage.* Their courage in trying out the Self-Pact provided the first inkling that: there was quite likely a range of Triggering emotions, transcending anger and rage per se, that were not previously recognized as such, and that . . . many of these categories of Triggering could *also* be harnessed and addressed in a salutary manner using the Self-Pact.

In other words . . . there was more to be revealed.

A small hint of this was visible in the final essay in *Anger and Rage Addiction & The Self-Pact:*

> "As the Self-Pact continues on to do its work as a healing catalyst in the lives of real people wrestling with Anger and Rage Addiction (*and, perhaps, with other afflictions of the human soul* [emphasis added]), so, too, may it

confer a dignity on the irrepressibility of the human psyche—ever striving for an increasing attainment of wholeness despite the presence—both within and without—of an array of obstructions and challenges that can appear to make the odds of arriving at wholeness seem very long, indeed."[3]

And so . . . with the Self-Pact four years along on its journey, there were already intimations surfacing that the conditions which could derive benefit from it might run far afield of just "anger and rage."

This brings us to the topic of "Behavioral Addictions."

Expanding the Paradigm

REGARDING MY OWN AWARENESS, the whole area of Behavioral Addictions, and its relevance to understanding what, at root, addictions of any stripe have in common in terms of the dynamics that propel them, started as a recognition of sex and 'love' addiction as a form of addiction that could exist *independent of active alcoholism and drug addiction.* In other words, sex and 'love' addiction(s) had its (their) own autonomous nature. This awareness had become clear to me by 1976, when I was sober in terms of active alcoholism for 5½ years. This awakening to the reality that "addiction" could exist outside the realm of where it was generally considered to be encountered, started a whole, long, odyssey for me. I returned to college (Goddard College in Plainfield, Vermont) in my early thirties, to pursue this fascination, which was buttressed by a senior thesis in which I, having read most all of Sigmund Freud's published works, searched for, and found, significant parallels between psychoanalytic thought and addiction theory. I was looking for larger linkages that could

---

3. Excerpted from *Anger and Rage Addiction & The Self-Pact,* pp. 107–108.

encompass both traditional views of psychopathology and addiction dynamics.

This was a very exciting time for me! (My previous "attempt" at University-level learning, some thirteen years earlier, had resulted in my dropping out of college due to active alcoholism.) In studying both sex addiction and 'love' addiction (they are SO interrelated!) as thoroughly as I did, a "short list" of criteria emerged that were diagnostic of the characteristics of sex and 'love' addiction, and, moreover, *were derived directly from the characteristics of active alcoholism and drug addiction.*

Here's what got boiled down, both through my studies at Goddard College, and subsequent masters degree studies as Harvard University:

The Five Diagnostic Criteria (for ALL Addictions)[4]

(NOTE: This list of criteria is derived directly from active alcoholism and drug addiction. It is applicable for diagnosing all addictions, whether substance-based or purely behavioral)

(1) Use of a substance or activity for the purpose of *enhancing pleasure* (either physical or psychological, or both) or *decreasing pain* (either physical, psychological, or both)—"energizing" or "sedating"—OR for the purpose of *maintaining the ability to function* (a Tolerance-related effect).

NOTE: key words and phrases for this criterion: enhancing pleasure, decreasing pain, maintaining ability to function, Tolerance.

---

4. This list of addiction criteria is taken from the version published in my book *Behavioral Addictions: A New Solution to Very Old Problems* (Four Rivers Press, 2016: available through: fourriverspress.com). The generic list was pretty much intact by 1982 or so.

(2) Over time, there is an *increasing amount of consumption or indulgence* required to achieve an acceptable level of "pay-off," or "return"—the development of Tolerance.

NOTE: key words and phrases for this criterion: increasing consumption, increasing indulgence, Tolerance, achieving "pay-off" or "return."

(3) *Loss of control* over rate, frequency and/or duration of consumption/indulgence.

Rate	How much "quantity" I'm doing when I indulge/act out.
Frequency	How often I'm acting out/indulging.
Duration	How long (temporally) an indulgence/acting-out episode lasts.

NOTE: key words and phrases for this criterion: loss of control, rate, frequency, duration.

(4) *Symptoms of withdrawal* (physical, psychological, emotional, spiritual, or any combination of the above) are encountered if consumption/indulgence, and access to "source of supply"/opportunities to act-out are abruptly curtailed (another Tolerance-related effect).

NOTE: key words and phrases for this criterion: withdrawal symptoms, Tolerance

(5) Progression: increasingly negative consequences accruing over time as a direct result of loss of control—life unmanageability.

NOTE: key words and phrases for this criterion: progression, negative consequences, life unmanageability[5]

---

5. It is reasonable to wonder why "blackouts," as a diagnostic symptom of

These criteria for addictions—*all* addictions—and the observations and experiences that birthed them, opened the gates for a whole, new, encompassing vantage point for assessing just what "addiction" consists of, in terms of its characteristics and (to speak clinically) what ramifications there might be regarding diagnosing *and* treating behavioral addictions—drawing on treatment approaches that were useful in addressing alcoholism and drug addiction.[6]

What is significant, from the standpoint of what this book seeks to address, is the discovery—even in hindsight—that *the phenomenology of Triggering is NOT limited to anger and rage addiction.* Notwithstanding the fact that anger and rage may constitute one of Triggering's most pronounced manifestations . . . in fact, Triggering exists at different levels and degrees of intensity

---

addiction, does not make the list of diagnostic criteria. Indeed, "blackouts," and other phenomena of dissociation, are not, infrequently, to be observed in addictions-prone individuals, including both substance-based and non-substance-based addictions. The reason that "blackouts" did not make the list is that "blackouts" are NOT a *universal* phenomenon in the manifestation of addictions-oriented behaviors. Hence, blackouts or "time-loss experiences," though not exactly rare, do not occur with sufficient frequency to make the list. But . . . one should certainly take note of the presence of dissociative symptoms in working with addictions-prone individuals. Very often, when "time-loss" experiences *are* in the picture, and regardless of whether such experiences are occurring to someone who is actively addicted or someone who is already clean and sober, a history of childhood trauma lurks in the background.

6. A full discussion regarding what treatment approaches, as derived from alcoholism and drug addiction treatment protocols, are useful for addressing behavioral addictions, is beyond the scope or intention of this book. However, for those who have a deeper interest in such matters, my book *Behavioral Addictions: A New Solution to Very Old Problems* (Four Rivers Press, 2016) sheds significant light on these matters.

across a very wide range of behaviors and their outworkings.[7]

And . . . in the interests of writing up a once-over survey of events leading up to the larger recognition of the ubiquity of "Triggering," there are a couple of subheadings in my own search for clarity on these matters that warrant mentioning. These may entail what appear to be a bit of a digression from the overall topic, but I promise you I will return to the main topic—the recognition of a wider panorama of the manifestation of Triggering—soon enough.

Digression and Return

SO HERE WE GO: A number of years ago (early 2000s) I was asked to teach a course on Behavioral Addictions—which, as you now know, had already been, and still is, a passionate topic for me. The opportunity to teach this course arose spontaneously, as I happened to receive an unsolicited piece of mail from an organization which, at the time, was called The New England School for Addiction Studies (consisting of a consortium of the bureaus of alcoholism/substance abuse and public health-related agencies in the six New England states). The piece of mail I received was really a promotional flier for the then-upcoming summer school (these were five-day June events), and the pro-

---

7. Much of what is designated here as "Triggering" does manifest in emotional surfacings that are substantially less in volume and intensity than, say, "anger and rage," jealousy, betrayal, heartbreak, etc. However, the appearance of the subtler ones, such as "worry," "concern," "suspicion" (among countless others), still manifest as autonomous arrisings, in which our everyday awareness *discovers* their presence, rather than creates their presence. To this extent, although the process of their presence may seem slower, the basic dynamic of Triggering still exists. Whether their arising is blatant or subtle, they are all emanations that are not initially known to ego consciousness (although they await their opportunity to become so).

gram that was listed included a course offering on "Behavioral Addictions."

My curiosity was piqued. Who, I wondered, would be the presenter for such a course (since I knew of no one else, other than me, who was covering this territory)? So . . . I got in touch with the NESAS (New England School for Addiction Studies) and, somewhat gingerly, inquired as to whether they had lined someone up to present the course. As it turned out, they had neither a course syllabus, nor anyone to develop one, let alone present it.

I offered my services. They said, "Send us a CV (curriculum vitae) along with a proposed course outline." I did. They said, "You're it." That was the start of a fifteen-year run of, annually, presenting the course on Behavioral Addictions, which came to include, over the years, a course on Anger and Rage Addiction and the Self-Pact, and a course on Sex and 'Love' Addiction. It was a good run, indeed!

One of the benefits of being teaching faculty at The New England School for Addiction Studies was that we could, ourselves, choose to attend other course offerings that struck our prospective fancies. This was a great plus for teaching there because, in any year of the School, the many courses offered ran a range from generic orientations, to highly specialized topics. In addition to my own teaching, I availed myself fully of the opportunity to attend other course offerings.

And . . . did I ever strike it rich!! In 2013, a course was offered under the heading: "Trauma Across the Lifespan."[8] The Self-Pact had already come into being four years earlier, and *Anger and Rage Addiction & The Self-Pact* had just been published. In my book I had already expressed a critique of then-current treatment approaches in "dealing with" anger and rage Triggering. The standard approaches were behavioral in nature, placing a premium on heading off Triggering by developing cognitive-

---

8. This exceptional course was taught by Linda Douglas, M.Ed., a counselor who, at the time, was working in Connecticut.

oriented defenses to keep it from occurring. As mentioned earlier, I had already, by this point, found evidence that attempting to head off Triggering was a futile act, because the neurology of Triggering (70ms) is so much quicker that the neurology of "becoming aware" that one has Triggered (470 ms)[9]—that by the time awareness of Triggering occurred, it's already "old news"— it happened ½ second earlier. Rational, well-intentioned consciousness was just too slow to "get out ahead of it."

Linda Douglass, M.Ed.'s course on trauma across the life-span served up another original contribution which deepened my comprehension of the futility of trying to squelch, or otherwise suppress, the phenomenon of Triggering.

Here it is (along with my gratitude to her for what she uncovered): Triggering is often considered a unitary event based on a particular, specific provocation, or catalyst. In the behavioral modification/mitigation/cognitive restructuring approaches to treatment, one identifies the "stimulus" (typically considered to be a singular source), develops awareness of the rising tenor that, if not headed off, will inexorably lead to a Triggering episode and its subsequent unleashings, and, then, consciously steers away from it, along with the unleashing and "acting out" which would inevitably follow.

Here's where the plot thickens: Would that we were occupying a world in which there are "single" catalysts for a Triggering episode. Even then (if that were so), it *might*, if we're really fortunate, be possible to "get out ahead of it" with our rational faculties and "head it off," or somehow divert our thought process (to the extent we're aware of it) away from it. Given the different speeds of the neurology involved with the actual event of Triggering and "becoming aware that I've Triggered," this possibility of intervening to head Triggering off is really a longshot—but, for the purpose of this discussion, let's hold, for the moment, to its being possible: a longshot, but still (maybe) possible.

---

9. Reference for this has already been cited. Please see footnote 3 on page 15.

Here's the crusher: It is usually the case that even single acts of Triggering have multi-sourced origins. For instance, in a trauma-Triggered scenario, in which current ego consciousness finds itself suddenly going over a cliff with Triggered torment, the catalyst-Triggering could be *anything*—and everything: the color of a wall, rendered patterns on wallpaper, the curl or curve on a bannister's railing, a particular color appearing in any environment, a certain taste, some seemingly random auditory stimulus (a song, a rumbling noise, a siren, a truck backfiring, wind wending through trees branches, raindrops landing on a roof or blowing against windows, and so on)—all nameless/originless (in the conscious mind of the person who's under assault)—a fancied glimpse of a particular silhouette while seeing the profile of someone's head, the particular gait of a person's walking, an article of clothing a person is wearing, feeling suddenly caught in someone's gaze, a specific kind of weather, clouds arrayed in various patterns in the sky, a particular time of day, a particular time of year, a particular calendar date . . . and on and on. Here's the rub: *Given a person's particular, specific trauma history, any and all of these catalytic sources (and countless more) are sufficient, individually as well as in concert, to launch Triggering.*

The inference that this example dramatizes is that achieving the mastery to be able to squelch or suppress a Triggering episode (if it were hypothetically possible to do so) would necessitate—*not* merely a way to intercept a Triggering episode as promulgated by a single unconscious source—but, rather, *a mastery of, and over, ALL*—each and every one—*of the possible intrapsychic stimuli*—most of which being unconscious to ego consciousness—that, both individually and collectively, constitute the multivariate resonances, sources, catalysts, for a Triggering episode.

It is humbly suggested that this task is not possible.

IN 2016 I PUBLISHED a follow-up book to *Anger and Rage Addiction & The Self-Pact.* Having taught courses for a number of years on the more generic topic of Behavioral Addictions, it was time to set something more definitive down in book form. The new book was titled: *Behavioral Addictions: A New Solution to Very Old Problems* (Four Rivers Press, 2016).

At the time of publication of the new book, *Anger and Rage Addiction & The Self-Pact* was now seven years old. Over those preceding years I had come to entrust it with my own process of personal discovery and growth—consisting of (maybe) some self-mastery of one sort or another, along with internal adventures and encounters, epiphanies of new (to me) ways of "knowing" more about the depths of my own personal history—and, yes, the ongoing utilization of the Self-Pact as a "default" setting for whenever, day in and day out, I would Trigger—*still* a repetitive, recurrent occurrence for me.

As, over many years, my perspectives on addictions, starting with my own active alcoholism while I was in my twenties, had expanded more and more into a comprehension of "Addiction Energy" and its manifestations across a vast behavioral spectrum, so too, gradually, over the more recent years following the Self-Pact's inauguration, the Self-Pact concept—and the growing awareness of the more widespread significance of Triggering—started to expand beyond the "anger and rage" phenomenon, revealing itself more and more as an identifiable reality across a range of addictions—and, increasingly, as a ubiquitous feature of generic human behavior.

Regarding the expanding utility of the Self-Pact, it is of more than passing interest to me, personally, to go back and see what mentions, in *Behavioral Addictions: A New Solution to Very Old Problems*, both directly and indirectly, point to this growing spectrum of awareness, relevance and applicability.

HERE ARE SOME EXAMPLES from *Behavioral Addictions:*

In a chapter titled "A First Approach to the Question of Healing," under the heading **"Rousable"/Triggerable"** (page 56), the following introductory line (also in **bold**) is:
"The Ability of Addiction Energy to trigger or rouse—to

'show up' anywhere and in any instant—*seizing upon any plane of human endeavor.*"
(NOTE: Italics emphasis added, otherwise punctuation is as it originally appeared.)

So there's one—a preview, in a way, of the larger recognition that wherever "Addiction Energy" shows up—"seizing upon any plane of human behavior," a potential opportunity for the Self-Pact to be utilized is also at the doorstep. "Any plane of human endeavor" is a broad swath, indeed!

Further on in that chapter (page 59), when healing models for the manifestations of "rousability" and Triggering are enumerated (a paragraph each is devoted to (1) exorcism, (2) integration, and (3) co-existence)—and, for the first time in print is mentioned, under (4), the following:

> *The Self-Pact model of cure*—This is a new approach which has shown some efficacy with anger and rage addiction, and *that may be more generally applicable across a range of Behavioral Addictions in which the phenomenon of triggering looms large as a precipitating factor in destructive episodes.* The Self-Pact is an *integrative* approach to working with Addiction Energy.

(NOTE: Punctuation and Emphases in this quote are as they originally appeared in *Behavioral Addictions*.)

Even further along in the same chapter (page 63), under the heading **SELF-LOATHING/SELF-HATRED: Felt about oneself, but often projected outwards onto the external world,** this descriptive paragraph follows:

> The implied cure is to develop the capacity—the 'inner muscle'—to stand fast—stay put—under the assault of this kind of self-trashing energy, and to learn to 'ride the energy' *inwards* (emphasis in original). In so doing one is put in touch with its origins—the original causes and conditions which have led to self-condemnation

and self-destructive expression. Getting in touch with primary causes and conditions helps to neutralize the negative expression of this energy, freeing it up to be drawn upon in more constructive ways.

Following the descriptive paragraph of "implied cures," reference is made to footnote #24 (in *Behavioral Addictions*). Here is how the footnote reads:

> This paragraph on 'cure' for the energy of self-hatred is a highly abbreviated setting forth of what is central to a new approach called the Self-Pact. This approach has already proven useful in dealing with the dynamics of 'triggering' phenomena so endemic to anger and rage addiction. It is thoroughly presented in *Anger and Rage Addiction & The Self-Pact: New Lights on an Old Nemesis* (Four Rivers Press, 2013. fourriverspress.com). The Self-Pact has considerable potential to address, and help, afflicted individuals work their way out of the maelstrom of destructiveness characterized by the phenomenon of 'triggering.' *Triggering, as a phenomenon, occurs across a range of addictions* (emphasis added). As of this writing, the possible fuller utility of the Self-Pact for addictions which, in addition to anger and rage addiction, have triggering as a significant part of their dynamic, has yet to be explored.

NOTE: With the exception of the added emphasis, as noted above, all the remaining punctuation is identical to the original.

The final Self-Pact-referenced entry in *Behavioral Addictions: A New Solution to Very Old Problems* is found in the chapter: "Extended Healing Possibilities." The chapter attempts to address the healing possibilities as they pertain to how one comes to terms (in some fashion) with "Addiction Energy"—seen as a construct that underlies, and fuels, all addictions. In section eight (8) on page 123, the heading is: *Healing from, or with, the Energy* (italics in original). Here is the content of this section:

> It's easy to personify Addiction Energy as, first, last, and foremost, a categorical foe. It seems like something we're always dealing with, and there's always hell to pay if we don't. And yet . . . this may not be the whole truth, for, if one drills down deep enough into the depths of Addiction Energy, one finds just . . . *ENERGY.* The 'Addiction' part of 'Addiction Energy' suggests that, in its origins, what starts as *ENERGY* in a raw, primal sense—an energy of vitality containing seeds of creation, destruction, and renewed creation, without which life would not be possible—becomes tainted, twisted and skewed into a direction of *negative outworkings only.* What this reality (if it is true) suggests is that as we engage with Addiction Energy in a conscious way, through (as previously mentioned) becoming *reconciled* to its presence and actively accepting the responsibility to *co-exist* with it, *Addiction Energy itself starts to change.* Our own healing, meager at the outset as it may seem, may, in some way, be mirrored by Addiction Energy's undergoing its own changes on 'its end.'
>
> There is no proof that this is the case, but there *is* anecdotal evidence of this dynamic. For instance, the process of coming to grips with Anger and Rage Addiction (one form of Behavioral Addiction), engaging with the phenomenon of triggering (which is such a characteristic of this addiction—and so many others) via a technique called the *Self-Pact*—in which the *ENERGY!!* of triggering is harnessed to facilitate inner journeying—*has clearly revealed that the destructive nature of Addiction Energy, when engaged in this fashion, can recast its role from destroyer to guide and teacher.*

(PLEASE NOTE: In the *Behavioral Addictions* book a marker for "Footnote #39" is placed at this point—and subsequently referenced below.) The above passage continues:

> This hopeful discovery makes real that 'healing,' so to speak, may, in the fullness of time, be a two-way street. *Even the fact of anecdotal evidence that Addiction Energy, under certain circumstances, can recast itself into serving a constructive role, is big news.*

A portion of "Footnote #39," referenced in the above passage, follows:

> Though originally worked out for Anger and Rage Addiction, the *Self-Pact* would appear to hold promise in addressing the triggering phenomena so prevalent among addictions generally. As of this writing, research into the *Self-Pact*'s possible efficacy in working consciously with the triggering aspects of Addiction Energy as it manifests in other Behavioral Addictions (and chemically-based ones, as well) belongs to the future.

(**Please Note**: The punctuation and italicized emphases in the previous two sections are as they appear in the original.)

What, in the above passage "belonged to the future" as viewed from the then-present year of 2016, has become, in 2021, the province of "NOW."

From "Hunch" to "Fact": The growing landscape of Triggering's recognized manifestations.

IN THE INTERVENING THREE YEARS between the publishing of *Anger and Rage Addiction and the Self-Pact* (2013) and *Behavioral Addictions* (2016), what started as the mention of a speculative "hunch"—that perhaps the Self-Pact would prove useful in addressing "other afflictions of the human soul"—a statement that was as tentative as it was daring—expanded into a grounded recognition that the phenomenon of Triggering is front-and-center in the launching and unleashing of many, many emotional pressures.

As has been previously mentioned, it's not surprising that anger and rage addiction was the first manifestation to surface that would lead to the establishing of the Self-Pact, due to the sensational, abreactive wallup of its manifestations. The urgency of dealing with such states mandated a full-on focus be directed to it. It was way too soon to recognize, let alone address, other possible manifestations—many of which operating at a less spectacular level—but . . . still "operative," nonetheless. This seemed far reaching in 2013, more declaratively possible in 2016[10], and now, in 2021, absolutely relevant and, for some of us, *necessary*.

---

10. In those early years of the Self-Pact—roughly 2009 to 2016—there were a number of people who "tried it on for size." For the most part they were not approaching the Self-Pact from a situation of desperation, so the incentive to try it was more out of curiosity than necessity. The first inklings of wider applicability of the Self-Pact were in anecdotal reports by these non-desperate participants, who related having awarenesses of other "Triggered" states and emotions. Also, in 2013, I had taught a course on "Anger and Rage Addiction and the Self-Pact." This course was structured to provide participants an opportunity to "sample" what it is like to "hold" an Energy attached to some undesirable circumstance or situation (a pet peeve, perhaps) and "travel inwards" with it to gain a sense of what "inner traveling" is like and where it might lead re: their respective discomforts. Again, no one engaged the process from a state of desperation or anguish. A number of course participants reported being surprised that the "discomfort-of-the-moment" led to an opening horizon of inner pathways, and then to recognition of heretofore "unconscious" events—events that had not been consciously held when these students, respectively, had chosen their specific discomfort they, on an individual basis, wanted to follow.

What follows is a list—fairly random in its presentation—of other Triggerings—Triggerable emotions—in addition to anger and rage. This list may seem arbitrary, and it is an incomplete one, for, as it turns out, the "fracture zones" in which the phenomenon of Triggering happens cover a very wide swath, indeed.

Bear in mind that each mentioned pathway of Triggering carries its own emotional valence. While the whole list may seem random—and perhaps a bit sophomoric—as you read each entry *give your mind a moment to calibrate, however briefly, to the word or phrase,* and see if any sensation surfaces in you as a result of dwelling, however briefly, on the specific word or phrase. Bear in mind that Emotion [E-Motion = Energy-in-*Motion*] may be blatant or subtle, and everything in between.

PLEASE NOTE: The words making up this list consist of nouns, adjectives, verbs, adverbs as well as participles and gerunds. These words are language's way of trying to corral and describe a range of Emotional realities that elude and transcend easy compartmentalizing into verbal, written language. Each one of these words and phrases has an attached, underlying Emotional valence that is specific to it. The truth is: There are more varied Emotional currents than there are words to describe them.

The list begins below.

A Sample of Triggering Pathways/Fracture Zones of Emotion

anger	dread	sorrow
rage/enraged	attraction	unhappy
crushes	intrigue	selfish(ness)
infatuation	guilt	relieved
secret passions	scorn/scorned	hopelessness
crushed	unknown feelings	despair
'love'-struck	abandoned	deserted

craving(s)

depression/deflation

desire

strange emotions

anguish

bliss

cruelty/being cruel

self-hatred

peace

anticipatory dread

bitterness

impelled

compulsion

inspiration/inspired

drunk/self-righteousness

determination

insecure/insecurity

envy

moods/mood swings

frightened/frightening

scared/scary

embarrassed

desperate

relieved

fright

unwell

intensity/intense

flight

not belonging

worried/worry

saved/safe passage

odious

quiet

misery/miserable

troubled

grief/grieving

excitement

fear

apprehensive

trauma/traumatized

panic (attacks)

verbally attacked

impotent rage

physically attacked

emotional surges

compelled

disappointment

slandered

vindictive (triumph)

fantasy/fantasizing

rejected

anxiety (attacks)

alone/aloneness

wistful

damaged goods

surprise/startled

dishonored

numb

ecstasy

deprivation

freed

liberated

freeze

blessed

lustful

concern

terror/terrified

abandoned

disillusioned

shock-wave

reactive events

worry

exhilaration

enthusiasm

cornered

heartbreak

trapped

hope

forced

serenity

obsession

courage

vilified

dejection

forlorn

attractive

repulsion

indicted

jealousy

menacing

ambiguity

melancholy

elation

impatient

remorse

cursed

no escape

damned

inadequate

caged

gross-outs

left out

enthralling

lonely

under duress

"blocks"(all sorts)	remorse/remorseful	fleeing
afraid	horrors	indecision
regret	reverence	trapped
chase/being chased	raw fear	being stalked
dashed/dashed hopes	curiosity	bewildered
betrayal	hurt	getting high
lost	the Void	pain
threatened/threatening	possessed	doleful
broken romance	inner peace	bloodlust
sad/sadness	concern	longing
emotional ache	criticised	neglected

The Emotional escarpment is very varied, indeed! Bear in mind that while these fracture zones for Triggering are listed as specific, individual zones, nature is seldom kind enough to accommodate our quest for reliable, orderly, segregated manifestations of events. The reality seems to be that *any number of these fracture zones—not limited to the ones labeled in the "sample" list, but also sourcing from vast, untrammeled regions and history of the human unconscious—can "cross-hatch," or otherwise meld/combine, and, in so doing, create a much more varied, and nuanced presentation of the "Emotional mix."* As initial, Emotional waves coming at one another from different "directions"—different "angles," perhaps "phases"—maybe, even, different dimensions—they create their own wave-like "interference patterns," leading to amplified peaks, attenuated, hollowed out troughs or valleys, along with "standing waves"—complete with their illusion of being, for the moment, a stationary, stable amalgam of different Emotions—all happening at once. The manifestations of Emotion [$\underline{E}$-$\underline{M}$otion = $\underline{E}$nergy-in-$\underline{M}$otion] are robust, indeed!

So . . . the plot thickens yet again. It now appears that Emotions of great blatancy *and* subtlety are all part of the stew of being human, and each one of us has an individual history that can selectively amplify or attenuate them (or both)—depending on the pallet of available Emotional Energies.

What does all this have to do with the Self-Pact? Two lines of approach may cast some light on this question:

First, for those individuals (of whom I am one) who have initially entered into the Self-Pact because of having an ongoing history of destructiveness and mayhem, the Self-Pact has saved our butts. It has ceased the destruction of our marriages, families, friendships and professional careers, our standing in our various communities, and, in so doing, it has opened the door to our discovering and cultivating our own underlying truths—our own dignity.

As a degree of salvation in these aforementioned areas has taken hold—and, along with delivery from self-destruction, have been *realized* happenings—that is *not* the whole story. It is the "outer world" story, but (with the exception of personal dignity, which is a feature of both the outer and inner worlds), the "inner world" experiences are arising, and ongoing, for "riding the Energy inwards" has just begun.

And, for those who are approaching the Self-Pact out of desperation brought on by continued, untameable Triggerings of anger and rage, jealousy, hatred, envy, along with other assorted cravings and the like: the internal journey—a condition of the Self-Pact—continues onward, because Triggering, in these various spheres of Emotional current, continues to occur—only now there is the Self-Pact—available to redirect, cooperatively, the various Energies when they are Triggered (which is still a frequent occurrence, as would be expected).

Second, for those who have decided to enter into the Self-Pact who are not necessarily fueled by desperation, the adventure still awaits. While not dwelling too deeply on the listed entries of "fracture zones," it is likely that some specific entries on that list may resonate with inner experiences of Emotional upwelling—even if those upwellings are not necessarily massive, nor accompanied by recollections of specific occurrences, events or associations.

To the extent that they are perceived as, in any way, troublesome or inconvenient, those Energies from less catastrophic Triggering—but *still* Triggering—can *also* be consciously, purposefully held and worked with by way of "riding these Energies inwards."

Whether the Self-Pact is entered into through necessity, or less dire but still persistent emotional challenges—or, even, is entered into via a certain curiosity taking the form of a desire for deeper inner knowledge of self, the adventure awaits.[11]

So . . . what awaits us from recurrent, Triggered Energy and these ongoing, inner journeys with *us* as passengers?

Before we go too deeply "in," let's first consider some of the dynamics of the Triggering process itself, and how it distends and distorts our perception of outer world reality. For this purpose I'll once again use the fracture zone of "anger and rage" to describe these dynamics. However, these dynamics pertain across the board, to *any* Triggered Emotional Energy, along *any* fracture zone.

Let's begin: I am intentionally using *first person singular* grammar with which to present these dynamics. To use plural nouns and pronouns would, due to the ever-evolving vagaries of English grammar, add unnecessary complication to what needs to be conveyed.

So here goes.

First: "I" become aware that I've Triggered. Recall that the Triggering has already occurred—almost a half-second prior— by the time I am beginning to become aware of it. That may not sound like much, but the 460 milliseconds it takes just to *start* to become cognizant of having Triggered is over 6½ times slower than the 70 ms it takes for Triggering to occur. In "neurological time" that three hundred-ninety millisecond gap is, colloquially speaking, "large enough to drive a truck through."

So unbeknownst to me, "I" am already (have already been) in

---

11. Once again I do recommend, for those who are contemplating forming the Self-Pact, that you read closely and thoroughly the instructions in my book *Anger and Rage Addiction & The Self-Pact: New Lights on an Old Nemesis,* before embarking.

a Triggered state by the time I become aware of it—*but,* in my limited thought-frame and the slower neurology of becoming aware or "knowing," *I can only conclude (erroneously), that **my awareness** of being Triggered **is** the event of Triggering itself—rather than the true situation of having "awakened" after Triggering has already been launched and is now full-throttle.*

What's next? *I* think I've ***just*** Triggered (not true), so . . . I have to recognize—or invent—fabricate—the cause (provocation) of my Triggering. Since I'm ignorant as to the circumstance of having already Triggered before I'm aware of it, and therefore have *NO KNOWLEDGE* of what might be responsible for its launching from other contexts and domains of my personal history and unconscious life (of which I am also ignorant), and . . . knowing nothing about the existence of such contexts, "I" have to—***very*** quickly—size up my conscious/present situation to "discover," fabricate, invent, maybe even confabulate, *something* in my outer world situation that I can seize upon as an ex post facto ***provocation: the seized-upon "justification" for being Triggered.***

I *must* do this, for it is imperative that I justify my unleashing as being a wholly warranted and deserved response to an egregious, present-time provocation (rather than labelling it for what it truly is: a reactive ambush by my own unconsciousness's deep history).

So I *do* seize upon something—a cross word, perhaps?. . . a critical look? . . . an unfair (belittling) statement of some sort? . . . the mention of some key word unlocking some long standing argument or bitterness? . . . *Whatever may be seized upon in the outer world, it, in my impoverished state of mind (a.k.a my ignorance-based "reality") legitimizes, for me, my unloading of hostility and hatred upon my victim-of-the-moment.*

Sigmund Freud, such a shrewd observer of human behavior, recognized this behavioral tendency, and gave it a name: "secondary revision." He noted that we of humankind constantly crave a world, and its events, that are orderly, predictable, sequential, and (above all else) *rational.* When, according to Freud, we encounter circumstances and situations at odds with this craving for orderliness, we, utterly unaware of what we're up to, "invent" alleged circumstances to make any disruption seem, to our own conscious awareness, plausible, "called for," just, and orderly.

Returning to my "first person singular" narrative (following my Freudian digression), in seizing upon a plausible-sounding, outer world justification/provocation for "getting angry" or "getting a bit upset," I am completely—profoundly—unaware of the Triggering's occurrence *prior to my becoming aware of it*, along with *what actually Triggered it from within*, a sphere (as I have mentioned) of which I am ignorant. This is not to say, even remotely, that provocations do not occur in the outside world (duh!). All relationships include them and all partners to a relationship dish them out (at least in the eye of the beholder). *However, the deep-seated ones that Trigger from a state of which ego consciousness is, initially, utterly unaware, are generally much the more powerful than those spats that are (consciously) seized upon as "provocations" in the outer world.* The outer world provocations, in those instances when they actually occur, may serve as additional catalysts, and octane, for the unleashing that is already underway—but . . . short of being caught up in an actual situation of flight, flight or freeze (as in fighting for one's life) in the present moment, in which Triggering would be an almost completely reactive, instinctual event[12]—current "provocations" are

---

12. All Triggering has its origins in primordial, extreme, cumulative multigenerational life-threatening events, occurring over millennia, that have honed our neurology's instinct-based reactions. Within our own personal lifetimes, emergencies, desperate threats-to-life events and other dire situations draw on that imprint, and are met by instinct-based Triggering only. Unlike so much of the Triggering that is the focus of this book, which *does* involve participation of ego consciousness following suit on the moment instinctual Triggering has occurred, in "fighting for one's life" situations, *ego consciousness may be completely bypassed,* and the phenomenology of dissociation may take over entirely.

RARELY, if ever, the origins of the Triggering, nor do they, on their own terms, account for the octane, or fury, of what that Triggering delivers.

This is one of the main reasons that the "Triggered response" for anyone who has, for instance, anger and rage addiction, is so much "over the top" of what, to a sane responder, would appear to be a "provocation" (a slight, perhaps?), perceived as emanating from the outer world. However, the reality (as viewed by an impartial onlooker) of someone who has been ambushed by an overwhelming Triggering surge, is more like watching a person who is totally out of their mind, reactively seizing a shotgun—or a howitzer—to "deal with" a pesky mosquito.

This "reaching" for an instant, apparent provocation in the outer world often leads to a "rush" of vindictive triumph, and the experience of getting inwardly drunk on self-righteousness.[13] These ambient, unleashing states can also attach to other Triggerings involving different fracture zones and their Emotional concomitants, along with their associated, "invented" manifestations of dicey rationalizations as to "causes" and "provocations."

We are now at the next layer of comprehending what is going on with Triggering, and what it leads to.

Second: Here is the more encompassing story of what happens—the dynamic—of a full experience of Triggering and unleashing. We've already visited the territory in which Triggering has preceded awareness (always the case), and awareness is always late to the action—now caught-up in a riptide of victimizing, seizing upon/inventing/fabricating, the perceived "provocation" which, maybe or maybe not, having some shred of factual basis—and . . . laying waste, in righteous form, to the

---

13. I have coined the expression "the negative rush" to label the experiences of "getting off" on "lust for vindictive triumph," being "drunk on one's own self-righteousness," and engaging in acts of cruelty and self-hatred. A fuller discussion of this phenomenon can be found in *Anger and Rage Addiction & The Self-Pact.*

perceived enemy, infidel, or . . . whatever.

However, the truth of what is actually occurring goes deeper than this. There's more to the tale.

Simultaneous with becoming conscious and aware of unleashing, a projective lense—I call it the *Projective Filter*—is set in place as the portal and vehicle through which the newly Triggered/unleashing person (me, in this case) relates to the external, outer world reality. The Projective Filter is really an amazing construct, for it demystifies much of the behavior of Triggering and consequence.

The Projective Filter, as a portal through which the Triggered person relates to and interacts with the outer world, does this:

Regarding those energies and experiences in the outer world *that natively resonate* with a Triggered torment, the Projective Filter *AMPLIFIES* them. This creates an environment in which the supposed provocation, however real or fictional, becomes perceived as larger and more pressing than it actually is.

Regarding those energies and experiences residing in the outer world *that DO NOT natively resonate* with Triggered torments, *the Projective Filter distends and distorts these energies and experiences, making them appear as if they DO RESONATE with these torments. This leads to profound perceptual distortions and cognitive distortions that add fuel to the fire, collectively compelling the affected Triggered person (me, not all that many years ago) to conclude that the whole of external reality consists entirely, solely, of torments and provocations— a conclusion presenting itself as self-evident and obvious but . . .* **having been fashioned entirely by the distortions of the Projective Filter***, and convincingly delivered to the bedevilled, tormented person—is a "finding" that, regardless of presenting as completely self-evident, cinder-block simple, obvious and true, is, in fact absolutely, profoundly awry and incorrect.*

While the patinas of anger and rage, and the dramatic nature of their Triggerings, offer a useful, if stark, "way into" gaining a comprehension of the dynamics, and cerebral "loop-to-loops" of

Triggering, it's important to note that *these dynamics persist in all, and any, areas where Triggering occurs.* The felt onset of sadness, for instance, is always preceded by a Triggering—no matter how subdued and nuanced it may be. Just as in anger- and rage-beset Triggering, the Emotional tenor is already well launched and "happening" by the time awareness is turned in that direction. And, as in the previous example, ego consciousness will assume that the break-through moment of "becoming aware" *is* the incipient moment of sadness's being constellated—rather than the fact of ego consciousness's already being late for the arrival. All the haphazard "Emotional" terms somewhat clumsily listed on pp. 29–31, though each issuing its own, respective emotional hue, obey the same overall dynamic. It would seem that "consciousness" in the "here and now" is always "the last to know."

    When the Self-Pact is established and "in place," however, almost all of this—these distortions and distensions attributable to the Projective Filter—come to a stop. The "*almost*" part that continues, is the act of deep-seated—and deeply sourced—Triggering itself. Because it, in any of its fracture zones, is—due to its inherent, opportunistic reactivity—*so* quick—at the level it operates on (easily outpacing "us," our ego consciousness), Triggering, as an ongoing occurrence, and in the heat of the moment, cannot be stopped.

    But . . . with the Self-Pact in place, it **can** *be worked with.*

    This next section will delve into how, using the Self-Pact, that comes about, and where it may lead.

Working with the Energy: Using the Self-Pact

WITH THE RUEFUL RECOGNITION, and acceptance, of the fact that Triggering is "baked in the cake" of our neurology—part of our evolution-based inheritance acquired over countless millennia, and skewed, along the way by countless traumatic, desperate "fight, flight and freeze" experiences visited upon countless generations of our neurological forebears, as well as visited upon some number of *us* as traumatic occurrences in the earlier innings of our own individual lives—comes the recognition that, to have any chance of securing some deliverance from Triggering's destructive outworkings, we are obliged to tolerate its presence (there being, apparently, no other options). Having the Self-Pact as our guide, however, can lead us to some salutary developments that may even hold within them the possibility of finding a degree of peace and happiness. The adventure continues.

It is time to consider what Triggered Energy can do when it is being held in full potency, *NOT* unleashed on the outer world, and is no longer a party to, in a flash, installing the Projective Filter with its distentions and distortions pretzelizing our perception of the outer world in misleading, destructive, inaccurate ways.

Our Pact with ourselves has been activated. The act of Triggering—in the moment we become aware of it—has led to an immediately invoked (a tenet of the Self-Pact)—default into the Self-Pact matrix. Defaulting to the Self-Pact when one has become aware of having Triggered involves some inner-muscle building (a.k.a. discipline). Whatever the Energy Triggered in anger and/or rage, or whether Triggering has emanated from *any* other of the fracture zones (sadness, craving, anguish, anxiety, broken-heartedness, resentment, . . . and on and on . . .), it is always the case (as emphasized repeatedly), that our personal awareness of "having Triggered" *is* the late arrival to the phenomenon. *Hence, by the time we realize that Triggering has occurred it has likely ramped up some considerable momentum and stridency.* It takes a lot of practice with this tenet of the Self-Pact to instantly, and consistently, meet this already Triggered momentum with the conscious decision to immediately default to the Self-Pact. The development of this capacity is the intrapsychic equivalent of building a new capacity, and *it is necessary, for nothing further of a constructive nature can occur until this capacity has become operative and, a goodly percentage of the time, mastered.* In these matters teetering on the fulcrum of Unleashing Energy! can be dangerous! Therefore, the training of awakening consciousness to "instant-default"—which immediately activates the Self-Pact—putting us in "Self-Pact mode"—is of paramount importance.

Having defaulted instantly into Self-Pact mode, what's next? How do we "ride the Energy of Triggered torment(s)" inwards?

There are numerous ways to do it. Here are some (listed in no particular order). With the Triggered Energy held in full potency, you can close your eyes and open *yourself*—what you're concentrating on—to your body, and what it's feeling, and *where* it is feeling it. Having done so, you can "reach out"—in a quiet, inner-verbal way and address the Energy, acknowledging its presence, and asking it if there is somewhere on the inside it would like to take you to, or anything at all it would like you to know about—maybe by showing you something. You can say that you're willing and available to "ride inwards" with the Energy to see whatever it is it would like you to see, to feel whatever it would like you to feel, to experience fully whatever range of Emotions the Energy would like you to register, to have whatever "encounters" on the "inside" it would like you to have, to experience any kind of confrontations the Energy would like you to know about, to receive (and experience) anything: information/emotions/feelings/flashbacks/cognitive awarenesses/chronological memories/anything and everything pertaining to "original causes and conditions" from your childhood (even childhood facial tics!) or subsequent life epochs that have a bearing on your Triggered Energy of torment—which have led you to the Self-Pact by way of harnessing it "inwards," rather than directing something destructive with it "outwards."

In the above example I started with closing the eyes immediately following defaulting to the Self-Pact. However, there are numerous other ways to launch into inner traveling. Basically, any of the five body senses: taste, smell, touch (either emanating external to the body, or proprioceptive sensations emanating from within the body), hearing/auditory, visual (drawing on the neurological faculties of visual imaging with the eyes either open or shut), along with intuition/resonance (information transmitted by vibratory waves on many possible wavelengths)—ANY one or more of these senses can be the "way in" to initially "harnessing the Energy" of Emotion-based torment(s) and "riding it/them inwards."

You may have noticed that the quality of "thinking" was not included in the previous list. The reason this quality was passed over is because what passes for "thinking" is so pervasive—especially in its editorial modes—that, at times, it can be more of a hindrance than a help in inner traveling—at least until it gets tamed to survey (intellectually), rather than peremptorily judge or dismiss (intellectually), what "inner traveling" is starting to reveal.

No matter which sense you bring to bear via the Self-Pact to start an inner journey, the inquiries are essentially as listed above. Whatever "senses" you use to initiate an inner voyage in dialoguing with the Energy are up to you. Some will work better than others—individual differences account for this. With a bit of experimenting you can discover which modalities work best for you, perhaps even switching them around as the occasion may warrant.

Regardless of which senses provide the best avenues for you to embark on inner journeying, *the most important factor is your attitude. The seriousness with which you entered into the Self-Pact to begin with—likely, as for many of us, a product of dire necessity—will help assure that your forays into the realm of "original causes and conditions" will not be left unaddressed or unattended.*

While your framing of the inquiry you pose to the Triggered Energy as you travel inward with it may take the form of words/language presented as inner thoughts/thinking, it does not follow that the responses that come your way will necessarily arise in the form of verbal language. This *may* be the case, but many other channels exist for "communicating" information. In fact, while making inquiries is one way to engage Self-Pact inner traveling, it's also just fine to have no question or inquiry to make. One can enter a useful traveling experience with an open mind (and sensorium) and see what surfaces from the Energy itself—letting *it* set the agenda for what it wants to reveal— what it wants you to know.

There is no rule of thumb for how long a specific "riding inwards"/inner journey lasts. The Energy itself may hold the key to that outcome, in accordance with what *its* agenda is—what it wants you to know, take stock of, or experience. Often, in the inner-traveling state, a specific awareness regarding the deep past, and relevant to the immediate Triggering episode, will suddenly spring to consciousness. The startling effect of this may be all that transpires in a specific journey. The Triggered Energy response, having achieved its objective in making you aware of some "thing," or inner connection, from your past, which is new information for you, may, in that moment, be at the stage of "mission accomplished!!"

If this is the case, the tenor of the Energy you've been traveling with will, of its own volition, begin to subside, and you will be (once again) fully engaged with the "consensus reality" of the present moment. However, this re-engagement is likely to be of a different tenor from what it was at the moment you awakened to having Triggered, and defaulted to the Self-Pact. It is likely that the stridency and intensity of the Triggered Energy will have considerably abated. What, in former pre-Self-Pact times would have been perceived as a/*the* provocation supporting one's right to be destructive, or be a wet blanket, or killjoy, or holy slayer of the infidel . . . or any other outstanding manifestations of untreated Energy as it surfaced through any person's neurological/Emotional "fracture zones"—has become attenuated by the very real experience, however brief, of the linking of the inner traveling Energy to "original causes and conditions"— with "you" being both participant and witness. This connection has a primacy that trivializes, by contrast, whatever external provocations and rationalizations could have been held—and believed—as being the "primary cause" of having Triggered in the first place. A shaft of light, in the form of an *immersive experience*, has found its way to meet you (going at least halfway to do so), to connect you with what, unbeknownst to you, has always been in the picture. Now you don't just feel "something," enigmatically. You "*know* something," absolutely. The larger, inner journeying via the Self-Pact, as defaulted to during ongoing bouts of Triggering, has been launched. Through all this, no injury to anyone in the outer world has transpired. You and your Triggered Energy can both take a bow.

So . . . WHAT'S NEXT? . . . Answer: more of the same—except . . . it's never exactly the same. So many variables are at work, or "in play." One of the big variables involves how many "fracture zones"—the neurological channels, and the Emotional Energies specific to each one, that are capable, individually or in concert, of Triggering—you have. Most of us have many such fracture zones which are loaded with latent Triggers. We just, along the course of our lives, notice them as being individual, somewhat autonomous features of our emotional life, that we kind of figure we're "conscious about having," and regard them, somewhat casually, as "ours"—as belonging to us—rather than as Energies emanating from different aspects of our being, our history, most of which we don't even know we have. These are the Energies that influence us, rule us, even dominate us, without our being aware that, to a considerable degree, we live at their mercy.

The second set of variables involves *the specific qualities* of the Emotional Energy that *each* fracture zone has, and releases when Triggered. *Everyone is different in this respect.* The palette of Emotional experiences that issue from any single fracture zone is person-specific, ranging (speaking metaphorically), from hot embers, to slippery slime, to "frozen stuck," and on and on. You might, once again, want to consult the (far from complete) list of descriptive, Emotion-bearing words and phrases set forth on pp. 29–31—going through the list, one word or phrase at a time, in relaxed fashion, giving your soul and psyche the opportunity, over a batch of "seconds," to "hold" each word and phrase, providing each one the opportunity to make you aware of *any* emotional hue within you that attaches to one or more of the terms. Two factors in particular—the range of whatever fracture zones you may have (along with the Emotional contents that pertain to each one of them), *and* the specific Emotional signature you have regarding *your* own personal, conscious expression of Emotional Energy that ties specifically to each fracture zone—hint at the extraordinary panorama that "riding the Triggered Energy(ies) inwards"can cover in acquainting you, on more and more levels, with your own "original causes and conditions" that have, without your conscious consent, largely created who you *think* you are (in the absence of clueing you about "who or what *they* are").

As imposing as the prospect of ongoing inner journeying may seem, recall this: What makes it a necessity is the ongoing nature of Triggering itself. We haven't been cured of this. Patterns of Triggering—sudden, in-the-moment, unexpected, by ambush—are baked into our neurological developmental history, shaped by early-life events and all that has followed them. With such a background, *all such Triggering is to be expected.* The level of "success" (not a completely apt term under the circumstances) one experiences with Triggering has nothing to do with the fact that we Trigger, and *everything to do with having the Self-Pact to default to when Triggering has happened.* Then, with the instant default to the Self-Pact enacted, we, electively, *choose,* once again, to "ride the Energy of our Triggered torments inwards"—to discover, once again, where these Energies want to/need to lead us, and, once again, what additional realizations they want us to have, experience, encounter, awaken to.

So we keep going with it, knowing the necessity for so doing. And . . . while we continue to show up for these inward journeys, our lives, as we live them in the outer world, start to undergo a degree of transformation. Marriages and intimate relationships improve (at the very least, spouses and partners are no longer scapegoated wholesale); friendships become more earnest as we become able, and motivated, to talk about authentic aspects of our nature—maybe even our personal history—that we, for lack of knowing, would have been unable to speak about prior to forming our Self-Pact.

Those friendships which are geared to superficiality are likely to recede, as new friendships—more based on quality-of-Emotional life—start to come into focus, and take precedence. This transition is consistent with a change of values, in which societal, conventional measures of success ("getting what you want")— give way to discovering a *new fascination* with what constitutes happiness ("wanting what you have").

I made mention, awhile back, about how, pre-Self-Pact, the dynamics of Triggering, as soon as it breaches awareness, instantly results in the Projective Filter being snapped into place, in which outer world victims are perceived to have engaged in provocations that are instantly construed as making them suitable, and righteous, targets for our destructive, torment-laden outworkings. One of the most remarkable developments (and this can start quite early in the use of the Self-Pact) is that in holding the Triggered Energy in full potency, rather than unleashing it—the latter event (in the absence of the Self-Pact) typically spurred on by the distorted view of external reality as delivered by the Projective Filter—*the Projective Filter is **not** constellated! This fact bears repeating in more succinct form. Here it is: IF, having Triggered, and defaulted to the Self-Pact, we're holding Triggered Energy in full potency rather than unleashing it, **the Projective Filter will not launch!** Instead, we start to experience people in the outer world—both those to whom we are close as well as those who may, perhaps, be peripheral acquaintances— more as they truly, natively are—meaning: *minus our projections.* This formula: *Holding the Triggered Energy = Not Projecting It Outwards* upon the outer world—or, more generically stated, "feeling the feelings but not (re)acting on them"—seems quite straightforward, but begs disbelief in terms of just how profound, in doing this, this change in our perception of the outer world reality truly is, and what its ramifications are.

The truth seems to be that (prior to the Self-Pact) in our habitual unleashing of our own torments—whatever they may be—we have reflexively made attribution of punishment/reactive push-back as being deserved by those people who "offend" us—in the process, demonstrating our own defective knowledge of them, and who they are, which has been utterly whacked out of reality—denied and stomped on by our own Triggering nature. Their "villainous presence" in our lives is a product of our own disturbance. This is extremely hard to believe, let alone accept, because the distortions and distensions of the Projective Filter are *so* profoundly convincing that the "evil doings" of those we both love, adore, hate, despise, depend on, can't stand, etc., appear so absolutely real and beyond question—that we are locked fast in the embrace of such fraudulent convictions—having, typically, no incentive, or means, to ever question their origins or premises.

As I have earlier noted, this is not to say that those we know, love, adore, hate, despise, depend on, can't stand, have pet peeves with (and on and on), are not ever prone to being provocative in one way or another—maybe even on a semi-regular basis. It is, however, to say that if, through being Triggered, the Projective Filter is instantly constellated (virtually always the case), "we," in the heat of the situation, always strike back at our *perceived* tormentor. Our response is not one of measured, "limited correction" of a minor offense, *nor can it be* (in the heat of such a moment we are not capable of this!). Rather, it is, reactively, one of "slay the infidel," scorched-earth intention.

As difficult as it may appear to try out, the Self-Pact brings to awareness the true antecedents that have led to, and are behind, these misattributions of "provocations" on the part of those who—regardless of whatever actual "provocations" may or may not exist on their part—do *not* deserve to be misperceived as "the embodiment of evil," regardless of however compelling and "true" that assessment may *seem*, in the moment, to be to us.

The real test of this is when we are with someone we care

about—and *think* we know—and how, experiencing having Triggered, *we* (concurrent with invoking the Self-Pact and riding the Energy inwards) *actually behave towards these others by way of giving them the benefit of the doubt, i.e., that they are not trying to hurt or upset us—and see what happens.*

This is tough to do, for "justifiable victim," *through our eyes,* is "written all over them." What happens if, alongside (and after) our inner journey expedition of the moment, we treat these others at least neutrally—*not victimizing them?*

At first, we're likely to feel we've sold ourselves out, in not reacting to their (as we perceive it) "provocation." Every fiber of our being is itching and twitching "make them pay(!)," and . . . *we don't.* It's likely, in that moment, we'll feel utterly exposed to being victimized by our outer world perceived enemy of the moment, be it spouse, lover, child, friend, authority, principle, philosophy, bureaucracy, the weather, a co-worker, and on and on.

However, the discovery that comes from this tough experiment, if repeated enough times, is, generally speaking, this: *Our perceived (via the Projective Filter) tormentors are not consciously engaging in being our tormentors at all.*[14] They may be insensitive, discourteous and even tone-deaf at times in their comments and behaviours, *but they are not consciously out to destroy us.* They are, more likely, through having been, over time, *conditioned by our own unleashings upon them,* fearful of being hurt by *us,* and constantly walking on eggshells when they're in our presence.

In our ongoing Triggerings we may (and probably will) *feel* with great intensity and certainty what we take to be their intention to hurt us, but if we (via the Self-Pact) hold back on our perceived need—self-styled holy right—to retaliate, we are, over time, likely to be in for a surprise.

---

14. This is generally the case, especially among those who know us well, love us and depend on us. However, society-at-large consists of many exceptions to this, and it would be incorrect not to acknowledge this. On balance, though, I take what I have outlined above to be *generally* true.

Even within an episode when we are Triggered, but do not strike back, someone who is near and dear to us may make, on their own initiative, a heartfelt, comment directed to, and *about*, us, likely regarding something we've done (or NOT done!), or expressing appreciation about some aspect of our behavior that we have not realized was even being noticed by them. In other words, they are starting to notice us for the person we're starting to become, and . . . we are also starting to see them as who they really are. In short, we are commencing to receive a wonderful, unanticipated dividend for the very demanding work, via the Self-Pact, we've been doing for ourselves.

My own odyssey with the Self-Pact: Learning to coexist with the reality of Triggering

IT IS TIME FOR ME to transition from writing about the Self-Pact, and Self-Pact perspectives at a more general level, to something of my own eleven-plus years experience with it. I do understand that the more specific I get about sharing my own endeavors with the Self-Pact, the less generalizable they may become, and I certainly am aware that a quantifying subject of "one" (1) is not, in any research paradigm with which I am familiar, considered to be "statistically significant."

Nevertheless, I need to continue, at least for a while, in this vein of more personal writing because, hopefully, this line of approach, for what it lacks in statistical rigor, manages to make up for that deficiency through being more robust in its *resonance*. Subjectivity is good for that, I suppose.

I'll start by saying that, as I write this amidst a pandemic that leaves no one unscathed, I am within about 6 weeks (one day at a time) of reaching the slalom gate marking 50 years of continuous sobriety re: alcoholism and drug addiction. I got sober when I was 24; I am now 74 years old.

When I originally got sober I was purely ignorant, yet teachable—in hindsight, not a bad combination of qualities to have.

Not surprisingly, I thought that my own alcoholism was a stand-alone problem, and, in addressing it, I concluded that my life would be clear sailing from that point on. How little did I know!!

When I was sober about 5½ years I got into a lot of behavioral trouble. Activities in the area of conplusive sexual behavior and obsessive/intrigue-oriented, intense Emotional behaviors (now known, collectively, as "sex and 'love' addiction"), led to consequences that had me fearing for my sanity. I experienced being in the grip of authentic terror.

In the era I "came of age" (in my case, that translates as: "remained a child for an unconscionably long time"), there had been a tremendous atmosphere of go-for-broke permissiveness about this range of behaviors. The Vietnam War was raging, racism was being called out for what it was then (and, lamentably, still is), collectively inflaming the alertness of those who could "smell a rat" in what the U.S. government was up to. As Bob Dylan noted, "You don't need a weatherman to know which way the wind blows." The birth control pill was newly invented and widely available, so unwanted pregnancy was a thing of the past. Psychedelics were also bursting upon the scene, in lockstep with Timothy Leary's admonition (and encouragement) to "turn on, tune in, drop out." Tetracycline and Gantrisin, two major antibiotics for combating sexually transmitted disease(s), were newly arrived. (AIDS was beyond the far horizon; Hepatitis C was around, but no one knew it.) I used the VD clinics in a manner parallel to an alcoholic's checking into a detox center to get "spin-dried" and released, and then getting back on the street as soon as possible—no recovery there—"gotta keep making my game!"

In hindsight, my getting sober from active alcoholism at that relatively young age consisted, in part, with making a pact (intrapsychically) with "the Devil" as I vaguely perceived Him. My part of the bargain: I really needed to get sober re: my alcoholic drinking. But . . . *I knew I could not do this unless I could continue to engage in other escapist behaviors: particularly sexual adventuring and romantic intrigue.* It's true that I invoked a higher Power's help to achieve nominal sobriety in terms of alcohol, but . . . I consciously cut a deal with the the Devil's presence to make it possible for me to achieve *that* kind of sobriety (re: my alcoholism) by ALSO making it possible for me to *continue to indulge myself in other areas with complete abandon—continuing to live by the principle (as, at the time, the Joseph Schlitz Brewing Company would affirm for me in a pervasive advertising campaign): "You only go around once in life, so you've got to grab for all the 'gusto' you can!"* The simple truth, so clear in hindsight, was this: *Some part of me knew that if I had to surrender indulging in a number of other addictions which, collectively, formed, at that time, my near-total identity, my ego consciousness could not have withstood it. I would have had a psychotic break.* To avoid that terrifying possibility, I had to "make the deal."

The immediate outcome of all this, in unminced words, came down to this: "Getting sober and clean" off of alcohol and substances, rather than being a complete surrender to, and of, my addictive nature, was a half-assed, provisional, quasi, semi-fraudulent, *conditional* surrender in which I would continue to "act out" in other areas—areas that I took to be my generational, "baby-boomer" birthright (given the cultural conditions I have already articulated)—ceaselessly on the hunt for oblivion-laced immersions and adventures wherever, and with whomever, I could find them. My identity— ("I," "me") had no other foundation. The Devil was patient, I figured, and, in meeting His end of the bargain by helping to provide me countless acting-out opportunities even while I was continuing to be a "sober alcoholic" (helping to make *that* kind of "sobriety" possible), He would calmly wait for me to be ripe for the plucking—or claiming. In summary, His part of the deal? . . . Allow me to get sober from active alcoholism by providing me plenty of opportunities to indulge elsewhere. Even as, in such a perverse arrangement, He would be "helping me out," He would also be biding His time, and then, as I went over an irreversible Emotional cliff in a convulsive loss of sanity . . . He would, finally and with finality, claim me. (Of course, as a pursuer of instant gratification and oblivion, I never really thought I'd have to pay up.)

With the throng of generational entitlement combined with a hatred of our duplicitous government and the society that gave it lip service (good grounds there for getting into self-righteous indignation—drunk on self-righteousness), alloyed with the "Summer of Love" (San Francisco, 1967), and the generational coming-of-age Woodstock Rock Festival (Bethel, New York, 1969), the psychedelics-fueled "hippie era"collectively calling for a re-engineering of human consciousness to be based on the principle of "Universal Love!!", I had plenty of camouflage available to obscure what I was really about: I *thought* of myself as a "New-Age hippie"; *what I really was,* during most of this time (I hadn't gotten sober just yet) was a "drunk with long hair."

As I HAVE PREVIOUSLY REPORTED, by the early 1970s, I was sober, but "what I was really about" hadn't changed much. My active alcoholism was, one day at a time, a thing of the past—but my tendencies to act out in other areas (a few of which I have mentioned)—ensured that in my getting sober as an alcoholic, I would not, in my ignorance, miss a beat in diving headlong into a range of equally addictive behaviors, *driven by the very Energy that had fueled my alcoholism and, in hindsight, had also, at an earlier time, fueled other addictions that **preceded** it.* Little did I know. My drinking had ceased—in that area, obsession and compulsion had "taken a hike"—but . . . my "tendencies" remained the same, in their thirst/thrust for different escapist playgrounds and different courtings of oblivion.

It was starting to be time for me to come out from behind the camouflage of my fancied, generational entitlement, and "get real"—however, as a wise person once said, "The Truth will set you free . . . but first it will make you miserable." Who wants to volunteer for that?!

With active alcoholism—the only addiction, aside from drug addiction (with which I had had a brief skirmish—alcohol won out) seemingly safely behind me—the way I had it figured, I was pretty much "home free." As previously mentioned, it was at about the 5½ year point of being sober (in alcoholism terms) that my ongoing addictive behavior (completely unrecognized as such), blew up in my face. This time it was not linked to an imbibed liquid or inhaled chemical. It was, as mentioned, in the realm of totally opportunistic and exploitative promiscuous behavior (later to be termed sex addiction) and "falling in love with falling in love" (later to be recognized as one of many stripes of 'love' addiction).

But . . . were these *real(ly)* addictions?—or, was I simply continuing to live out my self-styled "generational entitlement," as franchised, collectively, by "us," the baby-boomers, and denied, hypocritically, by the then-preceding "obedient generation?"

Having drunk my way out of a university when I was 22 (I told one of my professors I was thinking of "dropping out." His instant retort was, "Stephen, you don't even drop in.") I hated schools, universities, and everything I *thought* they stood for. But . . . seven years later, going through an agonizing withdrawal from my unruly sexual behavior and unprincipled "love"/intrigue behaviors (always the same trajectory: attraction, crush, intrigue, intensity [oblivion—if I could get there], dependency, betrayal, hatred, neediness . . . next!), about a year into this unanticipated area of recovery I got curious about whether addiction really *could* reside, and possibly prevail, in these non-alcoholic and substance-based areas.

Now in my early thirties, I gathered up some courage and approached a college to see if there was even the *slightest* chance that there could be *something* in returning to school for the likes of me. When I went in for an information interview, a part of me just wanted to bring a baseball bat along with me to hand over to the interviewer, saying, "Just get it over with quickly." I gave as honest a statement as I could, including a self-appraisal of who I was, what I was, and what I thought my interests *might* be. It was all extremely tentative and timid. My interviewer listened carefully to me, and, pausing for a long moment, he said "I think we can help you." Apparently, "he," and "they" were willing to believe in me at a time when I could barely believe in myself.[15]

My studies at college, after a nine-year hiatus from formal education, were all about addiction. I wanted to really plunge into the possibility that "sex addicton," and "'love' addiction" (given that I had obsessive/compulsive problems in both areas), actually were *real*—and maybe, even, two sides of the same coin. This was in the fall of 1977. Moreover, expanding my focus, I wanted to see if there *might* be specific criteria that would encompass *both* substance-based and behavioral addictions— that might corroborate the possibility that substance/alcohol-based and behavioral-based addictions are "birds of a feather" and (pardon the mixed metaphor) "cut from the same piece of cloth."

It was an exciting time for me personally, because I discovered I do have a mind (having been taught, as a child, that I was a "shit for brains" and would never amount to anything). Also, there was nothing out there on the map in the academic world that had anything expressly to do with "sex addiction," or "'love' addiction," or . . . "behavioral addictions" as existing, let alone warranting, having their own rightful categories. It was all virginal territory!

The research I was doing was stimulating to me. With no other "current" scholarship in an otherwise unrecognized field, I plunged into an exhaustive reading of Sigmund Freud's major works, seeing if psychoanalytic theory and concepts had anything to offer that might further my understanding in the addictions realm. I was hoping to discover equivalent dynamics

15. I am forever grateful to Goddard College for bestowing on me the grace of believing in me.

to addiction in some behavioral syndromes ("disorders," in the lingo of psychiatry), that are described using a wide range of terms—in the absence of the term "addiction"—to label them. This was my first truly academic research, and it proved very enlightening. My senior thesis included a long monograph exploring the applicability of psychoanalysis to addiction theory.[16] The whole experience was like being a cross-country skier, breaking trail through virginal powder snow across a wide-open, ever expanding field.

All this time I was maintaining my sobriety, including abstaining in these relatively new areas of addiction I had recognized in myself. The longer I was staying "clean and sober" in these areas, the more I noticed that, though not specified, their existence could be discerned, *implicitly*, in some of the formal work of other academics, psychologist and psychiatrists, and noted **_explicitly_** in the lives of so many people around me who were living out/ acting out these patterns, *in the absence of any self-awareness as to their origins and consequences.* The ubiquitous presence of these behaviors, having identified them in myself, and now sensitized to observe them in others, was mind-blowing.

Following my graduation from Goddard College, I (much to my amazement) was accepted into a masters degree program at Harvard. The intellectual texture there was simply amazing, and I was most fortunate to slalom my way into some courses that have continued to enrich me over the past forty-plus years since I graduated from there. During my time at Harvard, I also had a supervised clinical internship at a gay/lesbian mental health center in Boston. Lamentably, HIV/Aids was just starting to surface; in the clients I saw, sex addiction was rampant, and becoming more and more lethal.[17]

---

16. I also included a fair amount of Carl Gustav Jung's Analytical Psychology in my studies. (I had already read quite a bit of Jung prior to returning to college.)

17. In hindsight, what is so poignant about this 20-year period (1960–1980),

After my Harvard days concluded (I graduated!) I was in the job market (family of four to support). The job market was pretty tight, but I finally landed a position as staff psychologist at an addictions treatment hospital, and, after about three years at that job, I got hired, also as staff psychologist *and* director of alcohol- and addictions-related treatment services at a community mental health center, where I worked for another three-plus years.

The clinical experience derived from these foundational years of practice was both broad and deep. Working with so many clients with such diverse diagnoses helped me hone my skills in becoming aware of, and having the courage to diagnose, conditions that carried a lot of valence in the areas of compulsive sexual and emotional behaviors, dissociation, and trauma.

What was awakening to me was the fact that so many clients had traumatic backgrounds and were experiencing "time-loss" intervals in their daily lives. Mind you, these were people who, for the most part, *were already in recovery* and not, therefore, using alcohol or other substances to manage their day-to-day emotional lives, or less frequent sudden upwellings of trauma-rooted Emotion and associated somatic symptoms.

Here's one example of this: Anyone who works in the addictions treatment field (at least the field I was working in at the

---

when there appeared to be a lack of consequence for engaging in libertine sexual behavior, is . . . that this seemingly permanent immunity *did last only 20 years!* What felt (to many) like the arrival of the "promised land" of eternal sexual advenuring (no "commitment" required!), no unwanted pregnancy, consequence-free and guilt-free sex—rather than being the new reality, was, in fact, the outlier. With the arrival of highly drug-resistant strains of gonorrhea and herpes, the surfacing of HIV and the growing awareness of the prevalence of Hepatitis C, the "old" reality of "consequence," including lethality, that formerly attached to such explorations, reasserted itself with a vengeance. Indeed, the new, would-be edenic reality turned out to be the anomaly—a fool's paradise, a mirage—and the old reversion-to-the-norm reality of sex-related risk was the persistent, or real one.

time—1979-onwards) knows what a "blackout" is. For those of you who don't know, it goes like this: A blackout is *not*, necessarily, "passing out." A "blackout," as originally noted, is a state of amnesia occurring in someone who is inebriated, during which the body can remain active—meaning socially engaged, physically mobile and viable, capable of functioning within consensus reality—with a degree of competence that can pass for "normal," who, upon cessation of the "blackout," *has no prior awareness of anything that happened during the "blackout" interval*—which could be hours, and, in rare instances, days long.

The prevalence of the "blacking out" phenomenon while drinking alcohol (and/or using other compounds) is quite common. In fact, those alcoholics who are aware of the fact that they "black out," and upon re-awakening (read: re-assuming executive control over the body as the person who was "in the body" prior to "blacking-out") sometimes refer to "blackouts" as "time travel" experiences because of the "loss of time," as discovered by the body's initial occupant/ego consciousness.

So all that may seem well and good. *However . . . what I started to notice is that "blackouts," i.e., time-loss experiences, started to be reported by clientele I was seeing who were already sober and clean.* I was amazed at this—knowing, at the time, of the term "dissociation," but not expecting that I would witness it in several clients at the community mental health center. And . . . once again, there was *nothing* in the professional literature—psychiatric literature or addictions-oriented literature—that made any mention of the phenomenon I had witnessed—SOBER BLACKOUTS.[18]

And this was just the beginning . . .

So, thus far, in my semi-biographical rendering, there are

18. I have often wondered, over the years, why I happened to notice this, along with other phenomena, while other clinicians had not. It all seemed manifestly obvious to me, and unapproachably abstruse to many others. Maybe they were trained "not to see."

several ingredients in play. Roughly speaking they are these: active alcoholism; getting into recovery from active alcoholism at a relatively young age; becoming "reachable" because of consequences stemming from other obsessive/compulsive behavioral syndromes (not yet, at the time, perceived as being "addictions"); hitting bottom and surrendering, as driven by states of terror and panic, as served up by my intense involvment with these other (now recognized) addictions in the behavioral realms (to wit: sex addiction, 'love' addiction); returning to school for reasons that (for the first time) actually made sense, i.e., I was *motivated*; gaining further knowledge in addictions due to my own recovery, through academic studies and research, intensive clinical training and education; holding positions of considerable responsibility, including being responsible for teaching and training other clinicians how to correctly diagnose and treat clients with "addictive disorders"; all this even as I was enlarging the scope of my own observations and knowledge, due to "noticing" new, not previously reported syndromes in "recovering," addictions-prone clients I was blessed to work with.

Out of all this, over a period of eight years of early clinical practice (roughly 1979–1987) came a growing conviction that Behavioral Addictions were prevalent, that they could be diagnosed using *specific criteria that were derived expressly from alcoholism and drug addiction—which, over time, I had come to rely on in my own work.* Also, the growing awareness of the prevalence of trauma histories in a significant percentage of those clients I had seen over the years, and the phenomenology of dissociation—"sober blackouts"—that I had witnessed and documented in clinical sessions, all started to stir into the mix.

THE YEAR WAS 1987. More was to come.

It was only a matter of time before the next wrinkle upheaved the clinical terrain. In hindsight it seems inevitable, but, back then, it was completely unexpected. The dissociation ("sober blackouts") present, and witnessed, in certain clients started to reveal different personalities—more helpfully referred to as alter personalities, or discrete "ego-states."

I wasn't eager to see this, for (once again) there was nothing in the addictions treatment literature of that era that cited *any* reports of this phenomenon. The literature that addressed "multiple personality disorder" spoke of the extreme rarity of this condition, and, no surprise, made no references that might relate "MPD" to active alcoholism and drug addiction, *let alone to those who were exhibiting dissociative symptoms who had a history of alcoholism and drug addiction, and who were already sober and clean—and in longer-term recovery from these addictions.*

By 1989, I had seen enough to realize that I could not deny the reality, and prevalence, of the phenomena I was witnessing, although, once again I wondered how and why it was that *I* was seeing it, and other clinicians in various human services disciplines—the helping professions consisting of psychiatrists, psychologists, social workers, mental health counselors and addictions counselors—were not.

With the intention of "pinging" the addictions treatment field—alerting the field of these findings, and the possible, more wide-spread prevalence of these conditions in other practitioners' caseloads (not just mine!)—I wrote a brief monograph reporting these findings. By this time (1990) I had noticed clinically significant dissociation in about 56 clients, and a subset of symptoms consistent with Multiple Personality Disorder (now termed Dissociative Identity Disorder), in approximately 10% of them. *Further number crunching supported the conclusion that about half of a recovering alcoholism and drug addiction population gave evidence of experiencing clinically significant dissociation, and about 1 in 20, or 5% of a **recovering** addic*tions-prone population exhibited symptoms consistent with MPD/DID.

This brief article was published in *The Counselor,* at that time a monthly periodical published by the National Association of Alcoholism and Drug Abuse Counselors (NAADAC), in

1990.[19] Over the months that followed publication I received but one response from a person who thought I was running a program for treatment of MPD (which I wasn't). Aside from this, no other communications or inquiries were to be had regarding this article and its reported findings. The addictions treatment field's self-limiting areas of concern, exclusively focused on alcoholism and drug addiction, remained "unaltered"—the field was still asleep, and it appeared to have a vested interest in remaining so . . .

THE FIELD MAY HAVE CONTINUED to snooze, but I did not. My interests and my own learning were continuing apace. The next major cog in the gearworks was about to come into the foreground. It's called "Triggering."

"Triggering" was not a term in common professional use in 1990. It was more a colloquial term, occasionally surfacing as a self-reported syndrome. There was, as of yet, no melding of concepts in a manner that would indicate common ground occupied by experiences such as shell-shock; dissociation; alcoholism and drug addiction—the phenomenon of craving; other cravings (of all sorts); survivors of childhood incest, sexual abuse, physical abuse, sadism and deprivation; traumatic events as in catastrophic loss; domestic violence/crimes of passion; post-traumatic stress disorder (PTSD), and so on.

There was the diagnosis of "borderline personality disorder"— at the time a one-size-fits-all catch-basin/catch-all diagnosis that centered on the highly labile presentation of fractured

---

19. As of this writing, 31 years have passed since this article was published. I have not yet been successful in locating, after all these years, the specific month in 1990 when my article was published in "The Counselor."
I contacted NAADAC about purchasing the issue containing my article, however, lamentably, whatever archive may exist at NAADAC does not extend back to 1990.

Emotional states and moods (and "opinions!"), swinging, without prior notice, quickly back and forth between polar opposites of intense Emotional feeling. This diagnosis was very popular and, frankly, greatly overused in its heyday (1980s).

It took until the early 1990s for the bridges to be crossed that connected the Emotional lability of "borderline personality disorder" with traumatic antecedents, be they war/combat related ("shell shock"), childhood related, domestic violence/crimes of passion related, criminality related, etc. Eventually all of these sources and manifestations of traumatic underpinnings started to meld under the much more useful, and responsibly inclusive, diagnosis and attribution: "Post-Traumatic Stress." *Diagnoses such as "borderline personality disorder," which, along with a batch of others, articulated observed specific behaviors, were subsumed, for the first time, with a diagnosis that pointed to* **cause,** *rather than just highlighting behavioral symptoms.*

At least, over time, "borderline personality disorder"—that diagnosis that perseveratively looked at surface (behavioral) symptoms rather than concerning itself with the provenance—the root causes—of such behaviors—deservedly receded more into the background, and new (and some very old) diagnoses started to come into the foreground (once again) that were more causation-focused, rather than one-dimensional "behavioral-symptoms" focused. *Additionally, the possibility that "disorder" may be more fruitfully considered and addressed as "adaptation" rather than as pathology—extraordinary adaptive responses to excruciating circumstances—began to gain a bit of traction.*[20]

As the terms "Triggers" and "Triggering" commenced, following their grass roots origins, to come into more frequent usage among human services providers, attention became more and more focused on how these phenomena relate to a deeper

---

20. Whether the term "Post-Traumatic Stress" is more fruitfully considered an adaptation rather than a disorder (with its inference of pathology) is a matter that still, after all these years, gets debated.

history, and the role they play in determining a range of "adapta-tions" stemming from traumatic events. Much of this attention was also geared to recognizing Triggering's role as a catalyst for launching destructive behaviors.

For instance, in MPD/DID clients, where separate ego-states prevail—typically unbeknownst to the individual ego-state partici-pants (alter personalities) in such an arrangement—Triggering/being Triggered is often the sign of an immediate "switch" occurring from one ego state/alter personality to another. In the addictions realm the onset of craving is (usually) a Triggered event, as is blackout phenomena previously described. No surprise, anger and rage (especially rage, but often anger as well) are also Triggered phenomena that, as we have seen, instantaneously function to install the Projective Filter which, through its distortions, finds proximal cause and surfacy provocations for unleashing, with the prevailing ego consciousness—the presumed occupant of the body—being in complete ignorance of Triggering's provenance, underlying causes and conditions.

Additionally, all manner of moods, moodswings, menta-tions, emotional shock-waves, fantasies, desires, cravings, obsessions, compulsions, arousals, seductions—all of them involve a falling into a kind of amnesia that divorces a person from being consciously connected with (mindful of) possible consequences—*all these, and more, have "Triggering"—"being Triggered"—as common ground. Upon closer examination, one discovers that day by day, moment by moment, one walks through a forest of Triggers.*[21]

Thickening the plot—once again—came the recognition that in the various arenas and circumstances in which Triggering occurs, *it is almost always an entirely INVOLUNTARY ACT.* Even the subtler emotions of melancholy, sadness, wistfulness,

---

21. I wish to thank my dear friend Inigo Batterham, of Galway, Ireland for introducing me to the evocative expression "One walks through a forest of Triggers."

regret, dysphoria, ennui—along with many others—are also Triggered phenomena.[22]

With increasing awareness of the relevance of Triggering as a clinical/behavioral feature in so many syndromes falling under the heading of "disorders," various therapies were cobbled up to "treat" Triggering. By and large these consisted of various "trainings" of personal consciousness to become aware of the intrapsychical, and somatic, build-ups that were seen as the situational forebears of Triggering episodes. In these various approaches, "Triggering" was the perceived enemy, and was to be headed off, squashed, restrained, stymied, buried, or otherwise depotentiated by the building up of acute self-observation and "mental muscle." The perceived neutral (i.e., safe) state was the non-Triggered state, and all efforts were directed to cultivate such a safe, impenetrable ANCHORAGE.

It was really a percentage ball game that was developing with all this. Diminution of the frequency of Triggerings was seen as worthy improvement, although the goal remained that of categorical cessation of Triggering, period. There were "tools" for achieving this. In the addictions sphere, intercepting the presumed build up for Triggering was another way of "attacking" the sudden onset of craving—a Triggered phenomenon. In the DID (Dissociative Identity 'Disorder') treatment world—though I greatly prefer the more compassionate diagnostic expression Dissociative Identity 'Adaptation'—an attempt to intervene in the process of alter switching by allying (on the part of the therapist) with a "cooperative and sympathetic" alter in trying to build up psychical power to suppress—maybe, even, in the interests of imposing behavioral conformity—*to eliminate* the present

---

22. One easy way to sample this—the subtleties of Triggering—is to, upon awakening after a night's sleep, take an immediate sounding on how you feel, i.e. . . what Emotion is *already* in place greeting you as you awaken? Whatever it may be, the Emotion has very likely been in place for a while, patiently awaiting your awakening moment.

machinations—and even the existence—of a "trouble-maker" alter was, in some quarters, seen as a worthy goal and, if *appearing* to have been accomplished, a tactical victory (though there is always hell to pay for doing something that stupid and heavy-handed). Eating Disorders (often very close kin to previously mentioned conditions) also were prone to similar behavioral interventions, in which desires and cravings could, so the theory went, be fought off by similar means. The anti-Triggering therapies, with the "here and now" focus on behavioral results (in lockstep with a "managed care" system of third-party payers that demanded short-term treatments and documented case improvements to warrant clinicians being reimbursed for their services) generally did not consider traumatic antecedents—nor recognition of their significance to the conditions/behavioral syndromes they were ostensibly attempting to influence—as constituting grounds for treatment.

IN SHORT:

Right church: Yes, Triggering is prevalent and must be addressed.

Wrong pew: Behavioral focusing drawing on rationally-based procedures to address—and *suppress*—"disorders"/disruptive behaviors was out of focus, and (therefore) insufficient to the task.

For a number of years (fifteen years or so: 1993–2008) this is about where things stood in the behavioral modification techniques treatment world. And yes, it's time, at this point, for me to draw a little closer to my own narrative during these years.

Though sober from active alcoholism for many years, and behaviorally clean and sober re: what by this point was more commonly recognized and acknowledged as sex and 'love' addiction, my still undiagnosed anger and rage addiction (there was, as yet, no clinical diagnosis for anger and rage *addiction* to be found) was continuing to take its toll. My first marriage (lasting 25 years) came to an end. We grew apart, but my active anger and rage addiction contributed to the fact that we could not come to conciliatory, neutral ground and either rebuild our marriage, or part on cordial terms. It was all over.

Not knowing the dynamics of Triggering and the role these dynamics served in *determining* the battles I would find myself engaged in, my "condition" still existed, and was biding its time, just waiting to detonate again . . . and again . . . and again.

Post separation and divorce, my life simplified considerably. I was celibate for quite awhile (several years), and tried to digest, bit by bit, the extremeness of my losses: loss of spouse (whom I both loved and hated), loss of the precious daily rhythms of family life, loss of anchorage in the outer world. My life became very sad, and very quiescent—a life of subsistence dignity—somewhat monastic.

During this period my Triggering around anger and rage diminished considerably—though I wasn't intentionally monitoring it. Life had simply slowed down, and filled with the prolonged heartache of loss. I did manage, in 1996, to complete my doctoral dissertation (I'd been working on my Ph.D. for nine years at this point). I also started writing the first of what, over the next 25 years, would turn out to be a series of books—some clinical, some philosophical, some speculative. As a divorced man in my early 50s, suffering a difficult divorce, and with no obvious future awaiting me, this outlet of personal writing gave me some solace and sense of purpose.[23] I wasn't sure that I would survive my losses, but I felt an obligation to leave something in my 'wake' that could be useful to others.

My first book was called *When You Lose What You Can't Live Without: Identity Death and Renewal in the Wake of Calamity.* This was a soulful and rueful attempt to deal with the "actualness" of unanticipated human tragedy, along with the rites of passage

---

23. *When You Lose What You Can't Live Without: Identity Death and Renewal in the Wake of Calamity* (Four Rivers Press, 2009). Writing it (in 1996) helped me digest my "midlife demolition" losses.

that accompany it. Even as it helped me digest what I could, in very small lumps, barely swallow, I was responding to the realization that I might not survive the torments, but, as mentioned, I needed to leave a trail that might be of some succor—providing solace and at least a ray of hope—to those who are/have been/would, in their own time, be similarly afflicted. Writing it was cathartic; it helped anchor me. Other books would follow.

After living a solitary, celibate life for three-plus years, I started to emerge from my self-constructed chrysalis. I was not looking to "meet someone," and had plenty of well-grounded reasons to doubt that I could, or would, ever love again. And yet (much to my amazement), those Energies that had created me were not yet through with me. This is just a fancy way of saying "I met somebody."

In hindsight, I realize that the timing was right, and, much to my surprise, I was ready. In the previous post-marriage years I had not engaged in any alley-cat or "ambulatory-sewer" behaviors, so there was no self-disgust, with its resultant self-hatred, in the picture. I had been faithful in attending to my fate, whatever it might be. Emily was also clean, with no riff-raff or other emotional baggage in the form of stranded relationships (a.k.a. "unfinished business") or other intimacies weighing her down. We met on December 5th, 1998. We fell in love. Dawn, after "the dark night of the soul"—the alone, long, slow digesting of many hardships, indignities and losses—had indeed arrived.

Things were getting serious enough that I found myself wondering: "How long would it be before Triggering would start to show up in this new romance?" Without having much, if any, awareness about the dynamics of Triggering, per se, I did know that I had a "destructive gene" in me, along with a history of destruction to prove it. As Emily and I grew closer and closer together, one reaction within me kept haunting me—my capacity to "destroy." As a part of my prayer life, I came to include the following:

Dear Loving Presence/Unfathomable Mystery,
Please help me not to destroy my relationship with
Emily, despite my very real capacity to do so—*which
may even include my desire not to.*

In some sense, the acknowledgement I made to myself, for the first time—that there *was* a roulette-style process going on within me—minted a new awareness in which I came to recognize that even a fervent desire to *not* be destructive—a valid part of my nature—could, nonetheless, still be destined to destroy. Would new, untarnished love be enough . . . to offset the risk?

At least the acknowledgement of my vulnerability, as reflected in that emendation to my morning prayer, had happened. Admitting this to Emily, or anybody else, belonged, as yet, to the future. In the meantime (also meaning, in this case, a number of years)—largely due to Emily's love for me, her largess, her actually caring about me, and her gracious tendency in the direction of compassion—she demonstrated her love for me on a daily basis, her devotion affording me the time and opportunities to come to a deeper realization of my challenges, even as the risk of "destroying it all" still hung over me. I was, as yet, still in the phase of ignorance in which my Triggerings, acknowledged only indirectly as "having a reactive temperament" seemed (to me) as justified responses to (as I saw it) provocations external to me—giving me the right to be "pissed off!!!"

During this period I did read up on anger and rage and relationship dynamics. Cognitive restructuring was one approach (along with a number of others) I would "lean into" at times when I would come off of one of my vindictive triumph/self-righteousness Triggered highs (with its resultant Emotional trash strewn all about). Although these Triggered experiences kept me thinking—and wondering—what was "up" with me, I was beyond the help of rational, ostensibly salutary measures due (as I was to learn later) to the neurological discrepancy between Triggering, and becoming aware that "I have Triggered."

In one of my readings there was a particular point made about anger and rage unleashing that was both poignant and discouraging. The point was succinct and sharp. Stated simply, it goes like this: In the wake of an unleashing episode, the Emotions of remorse and regret may run very deep and be authentic and true—*in the moment*. However, for someone like me, who has a history of being Triggered *and* unleashing, the deeper truth is that such heartfelt confessions of regret, remorse, guilt and shame, as moving as they may be to the hearer (victim), *are merely stages in the process of reloading, in preparation for the next occurrence of Triggering and unleashing.*[24]

Not yet knowing anything deep enough about the dynamics of Triggering, I nonetheless took the above finding to heart, and strived to head off Triggerings, and . . . when that would fail, be authentically remorseful as its *own* gesture, rather than as a step in a "reloading" sequence. I was *determined* to tame my Emotional upwellings and destructiveness, regardless of the slim odds that I would be able to do so. With my relative lack of knowledge I stood about as much chance for success as someone who feels a sudden onset of diarrhea, and, with utter determination, tries to stop it by immediately "clamping down." (It ain't pretty.)

My intentions were good ones—heartfelt. My knowledge was still insufficient to make good on them. I didn't know the full extent of what I was up against.

So the Triggerings, including occasional ones that actually reached a destructive pitch—meaning relationship/marriage: verbal abuse and harangues—continued to happen, despite my best, most conscious efforts to *squelch* them.

In 2006 or so, I had at least a minor-league revelation that

---

24. I wish to credit *Vicious Circles Manual for Men* (Stephen C. Simmer, Ph.D., 1999) for helping sensitize me as to the role shame and anxiety play in the cyclical process of triggering, unleashing, and reloading.

took me aback, and surprised me. I realized—*felt it*, really (hence the "revelation" piece)—that I was filled with hatred—that *the Emotions of hatred and hating—were not, in this awareness, attributable to any singular person or occurrence per se, but were utterly global*, including all of humankind, and most, if not all, of the predominantly mountainous ignorance and destructiveness directly attributable to humankind's self-centered scheming, greed and the endless machinations in furtherance of influence peddling and power seeking.

I still could not make a *distinction between the hatred I was feeling*—as sourced (from what I could see) in what I regarded as the realness of what the external world, with humankind traipsing all over it, actually was like, and consisted of—*and the possibility* that I might be projecting as a stencil onto the outer world *what was actually sourced within my own personal history—a history I might not even know I had, and . . . a "projecting" I wouldn't even be aware I was doing.*

Curiously, along with the surfacing of my newly realized steady state of hatred, I also felt a bit excited—not in a rageful, or "aroused" way—but with having this kind of breakthrough revelation that I was not anticipating; the realization of the fact that I am a person who hates, had touched something deep inside me of which I had been unaware. In that moment, in a way that was therapeutic for me, I could "stand outside myself" and truly see *something* in me that was both real and perverse, and represented a nugget of new knowledge—of new *knowing!*

Was this new knowledge sufficient enough, in addition to the deep love I felt for Emily, to disarm the dynamics of Triggering—unleashing—destructiveness, that at times, I feared, continued to threaten our marriage and my aspired-to way of life? Not yet . . . but in hindsight I can see more clearly that things were moving in that direction—though they were yet to produce the conceptual Rubic's Cube-like twist that would make the substantial "taming"—resolving—of this anger and rage syndrome (as I thought of it then)—along with a number of other related syndromes that would become identifiable over the coming years—possible.

THE YEAR, IN THIS ACCOUNT, is now 2009. Emily and I had moved from the East Coast to San Francisco, and were exploring having a life there. A romantic, fabled spot (as attested to on postcards, films and in song), the environment—a climate of moods rather than seasons—was hard for me to adjust to. I never felt at home there.

The scenery, though, was spectacular, which was beautiful to behold—and at times, a catalyst for launching a wave of agoraphobia. I braved the outer Golden Gate waters off China Beach in Outer Richmond (where we lived), coached along by an older Ukrainian gentleman named Serge, who had already been through two coronary bypass operations, and who, as a self-prescribed medical treatment, swam in the Pacific off China Beach almost every day of the year. He coached me about braving the waters, and wearing a bathing cap—a bathing cap raises the *perceived* water temperature of the ocean by 3 degrees fahrenheit. That may not sound like much, but when you're in frigid, turbulent waters a three-degree difference feels huge!

My most memorable time braving the Pacific off China Beach was the unanticipated discovery that I was (suddenly) swimming with two weighty seals at very close range to me off that beach, even as a flock of large gray pelicans were skydiving the waters all around me (and the seals), going for their next meal. It was surreal.

I also befriended a couple of cats (Lucky and Zsa Zsa), two China Beach denizens. Actually, they scoped me out, and befriended me. Daily, over a number of months, they would wait for me to appear on the walkway leading down to that beach, and come sit next to me or on my lap when I would seek out the local bench (overlooking the ocean). They always saw me coming, and came out to greet me. At about the 6th month point of being delightfully ambushed by them, Lucky appeared, in good spirits, but . . . he was missing an eye. About a month later Zsa Zsa vanished entirely. They were outdoor kitties, but their guardians (whom I never met) had had overlays put on their front claws. This may have helped keep the home sofa from being ripped up, but it left Lucky and Zsa Zsa at a distinct disadvantage in the outer world. Nature took its course. They were my friends and I missed them.

The hazards of living in San Francisco I could not squelch: *earthquake risk* (if the collapsed buildings and the avalanches didn't get you, the gas fires probably would); *violence* (most every day in the *San Francisco Chronicle*, there were reports of random, spurious shootings/killings of innocent victims (their lives simply torn from them and their loves ones); *homelessness* (from the straggling, dissipated, barely ambulatory remains of those still seeking those gone-forever visionary days of 1965–1975 (as epitomized by the "Summer of Love" in 1967 et al), to numerous unfortunate people who had lost homes, jobs, marriages, partners, and livelihood, seeking surcease in drugs and alcohol (doing what it took to survive in Golden Gate Park); *poverty* (pervasive—set off with stark relief by the opulence of the well-heeled, in contrast with the desperation of those living hand-to-mouth, depending either entirely on the charity of passersby, or robbing those who had passed out on the walkways before they had located a hiding place to hole-up in).

To live in a pressure cooker like this undoubtedly tweaked my neurology to have a lower threshold for Triggering than was usual for me prior to moving to San Francisco. Numerous jaunts up to the beauty of Marin and sojourns into Stinson Beach (body surfing there), Bolinas ("the 'hippie' town that time forgot") and Point Reyes National Seashore lowered the volume somewhat (although "rogue, sneaker waves" along coastal beaches were also a threat—frequent, seaside deaths were reported to be due to this risk).

However . . . Emily was quite happy to be in the San Francisco Bay area. The environment of its (in places) pastoral beauty and climate reminded her of her early childhood in Sydney, Australia. Emily had landed a tenure track job at a university in San Francisco, which was going well, and I had a lot of consulting work (CISM/D—Critical Incident Stress Management/ Debriefing) with numerous corporations in San Francisco proper, Silicon Valley, East Bay and Northern tier cities like Santa Rosa. And . . . despite our separate "takes" on living in San Francisco, on balance we were doing well together.

Emily was coming up on her 40th birthday, and we were coming up on our 6th wedding anniversary. We decided to celebrate the pair (on a monthly calendar, these dates are only one day apart) by taking several days off, and immersing ourselves in the beauty of Yosemite National Park. We picked the first week of July, 2009, to take this celebratory jaunt.

The trip was amazing (you've likely heard it all before about Yosemite): spell-binding waterfalls off of half-mile-high ledges; mountain scenery that is beyond description in its immensity; trails that wander up into the High Sierra from a very closed-in valley floor; cascading gravity-driven streams with their provenance in the High Sierra racing downwards along pretzel-shaped watercourse ways—dashing to unite in the Mercer River; bountiful wildlife that finds a way to assert its "wildness" amidst human visitors. The whole place is beautiful, surreal, and . . . dangerous (a pulse-raising combination!).

On her actual birthday, Emily, defying her aversion to swimming in cold water, took an extended, blissful, baptismal bath in the upper Mercer river (even in July that water flow is sourced in the snow-melt of the upper reaches of the river).

After Emily's icy swim we rode some rapids on the Mercer in well-padded boats. Later, we tramped through some Sequoia forests, enchanted by the sheer stature, majesty and dignity of those ancient trees. We ate well; we had great accommodations, and we were very expressive of our love and appreciation for each other. What could be more wonderful? It was like rediscovering original courtship!!

After our run of days drew to a close, we drove back to San Francisco. Our trip away from the city—our sojourn with each other—had been beautiful, blissful, filled with spontaneity, soul-restoring—the depths of our love for each other was warm in our hearts ... and then we arrived home.

On-street parking in San Francisco is a nightmare. There are legal spaces *IF* you can find them at the hours you need them. No fun. In the house we lived in we did not have parking garage privileges. There was only one under-house parking spot, claimed by long-term tenants, so we always had to jockey around the neighborhood (often the "greater" neighborhood), which could easily involve, post-"getting lucky," a considerable trek back to the house. Even "getting lucky" with on-street parking had its downsides. We'd have to get up and out in the mornings, hiking out to wherever the car was parked (which, since the car was in a different location each night, required mnemonic agility to recall), then moving the car from its overnight spot by a certain time. As we found out the hard way, if we were even a minute late we'd be stuck with a big fine. (The "vehicular squid" were always phalanxing around during those fine-vulnerable hours, just waiting to pounce.)

However, this time (our arrival back to S.F.) our situation seemed easier. The other tenants were out of town, and they had graciously offered us the use of their garage space for a few days while they were away.

We weren't used to opening the garage door; we had never, prior to this, had any pretext for opening it. I asked Emily (or *thought* I had asked Emily) to go into the house, follow the steps down to the basement (where the garage was), and open it. I remained at the steering wheel. In hindsight, it became clear that she had heard something else from me, rather than what I recalled having said.

So ... I was waiting for the garage door to open, double-parked in the middle of the street (a definite no-no in San Francisco), and it wasn't opening ... and it wasn't opening ... and it wasn't opening. Several minutes later Emily appeared (wondering what I was up to). "I" Triggered—overflowing with rage and hatred—except, I didn't think about it like that. In fact, I barely thought at all. Rage had taken me over and I unleashed on her.[25] My serenity, love and gratitude around all the blessings we had, both individual and between us, were swept away in an orgasm of rage. The demon of vindictive triumph, combined with the delusional inebriation of self-righteousness filled me with a loathsome destructive power. The beauty of our time together at Yosemite receded as some kind of distant dream, or some old, golden memory that had put in a cameo appearance of "the good old days," and then vanished.

Amidst the tempest of Emotional and verbal abuse, I knew I was engaged in something destructive, and even started to realize that I was "getting off" on it (a condition which later came to be named "the negative rush"). Emily was stunned, Emotionally wounded . . . and "I" became almost speechless in the presence of such an attack that had spilled out through me.

As the stridency of my behavior and the symptoms within it started to slow down, *there was no relief.* Instead, a pall of grief seized me as I realized I had no control over what had just happened—no warning of its immanence, no sane, rational justification of any sort. I was a monster, and I could not cease from being a monster.

In all the episodes of this sort—from the most severe to those less severe than this one—but at times still threatening, at the very least, our bond together and, "at the very most," raising questions about whether we/our love, devotion, fidelity and commitment to each other could survive such an onslaught— Emily had rarely mentioned the whole question of whether my

---

25. You probably have figured out that this episode I am at pains to relate is actually: "The darkness before the dawn." You're right. The dynamics in play in this ultimate crescendo were age-old (as was my ignorance about them). That was about to change—radically. At this point in this episode, I still have *no* idea that, once Triggered, "I" was/am "the last to know."

destructiveness, despite our love for each other—could split us apart for keeps. There had been occasional musings about this, but nowhere near the pitch of finality.

Now, however, she didn't have to mention anything like this. It was already bouncing around my gelatinous brain—careening off the inner casing of my skull. My deepest fear was of losing her, and here I was in a situation in which I seemed uncontrollably hell-bent to "achieve" just that. I felt soul-sick, with no place to go, no resource to draw on, and nowhere to turn. Remorse gave way to *despair*, rushing in to possess the pathetic emptiness I had become. I knew that no apology from me was worth anything. What a fraudulent thing, in my case, an apology would be. I might be able to utter, so deceptively, "I promise it will never happen again." But *that* lacked any semblance of the real truth, and the *REAL* truth was this: "I promise I will never do it again—**unless** *I Trigger again (which, of course, I will)."*

IT WAS AGAINST THIS BACKDROP of despair, dismay, forlornness, and desperation that I had finally hit bottom. If nothing were to alter my course my life would wind up as pathetic—just another carcass cast upon the slag heap of the tragic—but not before I would have damaged the lives of those who loved me, or *had* loved me once upon a time, along with those unsuspecting children who would (having no say in the matter) have been infected by my toxicity—thereafter living out the damaging syndrome they had contracted from me—that I had transmitted to them—setting them up to have their own cruel, loss-ridden, tormented lives through which subsequent generations would be infected—and on and on it would go.

This seemingly unavoidable legacy was too terrifying and horrible to contemplate . . . *but I contemplated it, nonetheless.*

Yet, as far as I knew, there was nothing further to do—I had exhausted all resources of which I was aware.

Wholly desperate, I threw myself squarely at this dilemma.

Starting with the conviction that I was terminally fucked, even *cursed*, toxic, condemned, possessed, hopeless, despairing, I made a conscious effort to, once again, size things up, only . . . the landscape (mindscape) started to shift *ever so slightly*. A thought pierced me (I believe it was a Grace). It came through like this:

> *What if you start to consider 'Triggering' as the point of focus—as unavoidable—rather than something you attempt to keep from happening?*

The thought flooded across my brain—but it made no obvious sense to me. Yet, if Triggering *was* truly unavoidable, I began to realize that there was no other place from which to start—even if it seemed hopeless. But the suddenness of the penetrating thought, the essence of which was "Why don't you start with *Triggering as unavoidable?*" had caught me off guard, and I was momentarily intrigued with it. So I opened myself to whatever line of reasoning might follow, futile though it seemed likely to be. (There were plenty of precedents for that.) So . . . I ventured forth, not really expecting to find any form of deliverance.

Yet one awaited me, whether I knew it or not. It was what was to become known as "The Self-Pact."

The Birthing of the Self-Pact

THE WHOLE PRINCIPLE was/is elegantly simple: If Triggering is unavoidable—could not be reliably anticipated, squelched, suppressed, or otherwise headed off—*the starting line for any approach, good, bad, or indifferent, had to have something to do with the Energy itself.* As I opened myself further to where this train of thought was starting to take me, the distinction of the Triggered Energy as something to be unleashed—*always* the case prior to (and including) my latest demise—versus: the Triggered

Energy as something *that might be knowingly **held**, in full potency* (which, in me, was totally untested at the time), began to surface as a *possible* option. If (a **BIG** "IF") the Energy could be held, rather than unleashed, the victimization of those individuals—those I loved, who were nearest and dearest to me, and who also depended on me—*would be spared being wounded by me.*

But the *ENERGY!!* . . . If it *were* possible to "hold" it, would that be enough?. . . or merely one more futile attempt to contain it?

No, I realized. *Something had to transpire about the Energy itself.* **It needed to be actively engaged, not merely contained.** It needed to have a different mission than wreaking destruction on the outer world. What could this possibly be??

Simple geometry provided a possible answer. If unleashing outwards was *out,* and the ENERGY was present—and permitted to be so (no efforts to squelch it)—as in fully present in the here and now . . . *only one avenue of travel and expression was open to it: going **within**—moving/travelling inside.*

But did the Energy even give a rat's ass about doing so? . . . What would be "in it" for the Energy to travel inwards rather than unleash outwards? After all, it obviously was arising—emanating—*from* "inside." If it was, through its Triggered surfacings, trying to get out of there, why would it *ever* want to go back in? Who knew? The immediate operation (conundrum, really) that popped to mind was:

> **How can the ENERGY be engaged by 'me' in a manner in which it would be worth *its* while to try something like this?** *Would it be possible to establish some sort of accord between the ENERGY and me from which we might explore mutual interests, or causes?*

There was nothing left to try, of which I was aware, aside from this. This was the last house on the block—beyond that, there was nothing but wasteland . . . so I tried it.

It's hard to believe, as I write this, that all this happened over

11½ years ago. Everything about it is as vivid to me as if it happened yesterday. I made an offer to the Energy that if the Energy: He, She, It, They, "Whoever," or "Whatever," agreed not to unleash on the outer world—not create victims there—I would be *willing to be accepting of the Energy's presence,* and . . . I would be *willing to travel "inwards"* with His, Hers, Its, Their, "Whoever's," or "Whatever's" predilections—*anywhere on the "inside" that the Energy wanted to go,* and *I would be willing to experience anything on the inside that He, She, It, They, "Whoever," or "Whatever" wanted me to experience.* On my end, *I would not try to squelch or suffocate the vitality held by the ENERGY, and I would accept, and perhaps, over time, learn to welcome the presence of the ENERGY— its vitality, along with anything it needed to teach me, or show me, or reveal to me—as a part of my conscious life, even as my consciousness and awareness, would, perhaps, become a part of the Energy's life.*

Because, as far as I knew, there was no other option available to me to stem the destructive tide, engagement with the Energy had to be attempted; it was all I had left. This engagement needed to be codified in some way, and inaugurated through some manner of ceremony. *I started to realize, given all that was at stake, that the commitment was really a pact established between me and the Energy, the Energy and me—between "me" and "me."* With all that was riding on it, **the pact had to be sacred.** *Tending to it as completely as possible had to be the "priority of priorities." Harsh experience had shown me that any commitment falling short of a "sacred commitment" would not work—would not be enough.*

And so, that's how the Self-Pact was launched—no fanfare, no cerebral meanderings nor circumlocutions . . . just the deepest, most soulful commitment of which I was capable. Regardless of whether it would work or not, all that I had—the chump change of what was left of my character—got tossed onto the card table of fate and destiny, with me, hoping against hope, that, as I anted up this last time, I would be, somehow, dealt a good hand . . . and I was.

Early returns (1st three years) from using the Self-Pact

TAKING A BREAK from writing in this personal, somewhat autobiographical style I have been engaged in for a while, I would like to include some of what those early years (first three years or so) of inner journeying—riding the Energy inwards— began to yield, both in my own life and in what was reported by others who decided to give the Self-Pact a whirl. So here goes:

Because the Self-Pact is such a repetitive experience, especially for anyone who has anger and rage addiction (as you know by now, the affliction out of which the Self-Pact was originally birthed), the early benefits were immediate, and outer-world oriented: Unleashing and the victimizing of those in the outer world who were near and dear significantly abated. These early results started to support the hope that relationships which were hanging by a thread—on the brink of a final severing— were, despite all the previous damage, starting to—meagerly yet definitely—rejuvenate. This development, as mentioned, started to set in early in the Self-Pact process, possibly even before the harnessing of the Triggered Energy for inner traveling had proceeded very far. But . . . the omen of a possibility for forthcoming change in the Emotional climate was unmistakable. Something new was afoot. It was not, in any way, to be forced. It had to "come-of-age" in the fullness of its own time.

Of course, harnessing the Energy for the purpose of riding it inwards—honoring the deal made with the ENERGY to travel with it, along with the commitment to be completely available to go *"wherever"* the Energy wanted "me" to go, and to become aware of, and open to, *"whatever"* the Energy wanted "me" to know—had its own learning curve. But, *even with clumsy beginnings, these early travels had to be undertaken.* The ENERGY could not, nor would not (nor should not), remain dormant, or frozen, or trapped. It had to *"be in motion"*—to have opportunities to express its own realities and origins.

Those early adopters who inaugurated their own Self-Pact relationship had to figure out their own style for "traveling" inwards. Mine was simple (and still is): Upon becoming aware that I had Triggered, I would just close my eyes, and let my attention go to my whole body, as if I were riding in a subway car in the late evening, and the traveling lights were out. Establishing a comfort level in this state, I would relax and await proddings, from the Energy itself, of one sort of another— maybe spurious (seeming) thoughts, feelings, Emotions, cognitive awarenesses, chronological memories, anecdotes, flash-backs to specific scenes or environments, or to occurrences of one sort or another, and so on.

Others who tried the Self-Pact would write down whatever was surfacing for them "from the inside." Some would key in on a particular sensory capacity, be it sight, hearing, smell, taste, touch, intuition, and/or other sensory equivalents, such as Reso-nance, and let themselves be drawn by the Energy to whatever *sense* seemed relevant to follow in the moment.

Just the very act of honoring the Self-Pact commitment to "travel inwards" with the Triggered Energy, and then to exert oneself to do so as completely and devotedly as was, in that moment, possible, was enough to garner the Energy's attention, and start the "traveling inwards" process.

So far (as you have undoubtedly noticed I've unabashedly mentioned a number of times by now), the Self-Pact has been described largely in terms of anger and rage addiction—under-standable because the intensity of that affliction generated enough heat, misery and *necessity* to make the discovery of the Self-Pact, and its potential, possible. But . . . as time went on, it became clearer and clearer that the *rate* of the Triggerings them-selves, even with the Self-Pact well launched, honored and incorporated into everyday life, was not subsiding much, if at all. The possibility that the rate of the Triggering occurrences might lessen had been a hope, but, given past efforts, was not really expected, and was not set forth as a specific goal.

The Self-Pact had been predicated on experientially-based knowledge that Triggering had its own dynamic—sources and catalysts—*in motion* beneath the level of awareness in those of us who were bedeviled by it.

*Because of this, the Self-Pact carried with it the assumption that it needed to be effective in the **presence** of ongoing Triggering events—not as a strategy to ameliorate them.*

What this meant is that riding the Energy inwards would, because Triggerings, as expected, continued to happen, be an ongoing process of deepening self-awareness, as fostered by the Energy itself.

What started to emerge from the longer application of the Self-Pact was budding awareness—not just intellectual knowledge, but immersive experiences—revealing the reality that *there were other Emotions besides/in addition to, anger and rage, that also seemed to operate in a Triggering manner.* Sadness, for instance, might suddenly appear in awareness—but *it was not "awareness" that created sadness.* Again, sadness was a priori to becoming aware of it, with (likely) a similar lag-time between the actual Triggering, or arising, of "sadness Energy," and the awareness of "being sad." The Triggering of "fear," such a frequent and powerful Emotional experience for virtually all of us, had identical dynamics to anger and rage Triggerings, with the all important lag time between actual Triggering, and becoming aware of it.

In my earlier list of terms that have their own, individual Emotional valences (as listed on pp. 29–31)—some brash, some subtle; some piercing, some soothing—*every entry in that list is a product of Self-Pact inner traveling*—containing the first of many immersive encounters with *each* Emotion's "signature." That list consists of 159 Emotion-laden terms (and God only knows how many more Emotions warrant their own, individual designations), however . . . whether bold or subtle, each term appeared to abide by that earlier "anger and rage" Triggering/unleashing discovery. Each one appeared on its own terms, and in each instance "awareness" was the last to arrive—and had to catch up with whatever had already asserted its presence and was only subsequently being acknowledged by ego consciousness.

Over a period of time, various awarenesses were emerging from the inner travels in what seemed to be unrelated, piecemeal chronological memories, cognitive awarenesses, "flash!" moments from the deep past, sensory phenomena such as smells, mosaic or palimpsest visual images, excruciatingly fine details and "granularity" of deep-past moments (seemingly unrelated to anything already known or revealed), bodily responses and reactions and sensations (arising both external to the body and from within the body—proprioception), flashbacks of an episodic nature, the surfacing of a very rich palette of Emotional hues and intensities, gestalt experiences in which a total moment of childhood (or earlier!)—a totality of all its Emotional reality—would be presented in immersive, immaculate fashion—*all* these experiential/immersive/fine-grained fragments and random strips of torn Emotional and situational fabric, presented as something—*some things*—not just to be perused, but *an environment to be entered into* in order to absorb, on all levels, the truths that they held—all this, and more, were the internal manifestations and **re**arrangements of the spectrum of "riding-the-Energy-inwards" experiences.

Over time, it became clear that one's history, presented initially in shards and bits of multidimensional renderings—even if we could not know what they signified as a totality—*led to a realization that some kind of storyline might be in the process of being assembled for us—that our Energy of torments and perceived provocations, now turned inwards, was also committed to its part of the Self-Pact*—committed to making us aware of our own personal history—the story we didn't even know we had—fashioning for us a multifaceted narrative of who we are, where we came from, what happened to us along the way, and what, unbeknownst to us, had been driving us throughout the course of our lives—in which we were personally held accountable for patterns of behavior and consequences that, without our having any say in the matter, had been, unbidden, imposed on us.

IT SEEMS TIMELY TO INCLUDE HERE, in modified fashion, one of the sections from my earlier book *Anger and Rage Addiction & The Self-Pact: New Lights on an Old Nemesis*. Part of the task in writing that book was to attempt to capture in language some of the potentials that "riding the Energy inwards" could lead to. Verbal language is frustrating in this regard because one is attempting to take "torn-cloth" immersive, multidimensional experiences and render them a certain cohesiveness, notwithstanding the chopped-up confinement of words. This is highly frustrating to do, for in attempting to transpose direct, often complex, experiences into verbal language there is always something significant "lost in translation."

The following piece that I wrote for the earlier book, when the Self-Pact was only four years along, was an attempt to do this. So here it is (as slightly amended from the original). I hope it is helpful.[26]

---

26. The original section from which this presentation is adapted was oriented towards anger and rage addiction, the progenitor of the Self-Pact. By year 4, there were *hunches* that the Self-Pact might be relevant to Triggerings stemming from other Emotions in addition to anger and rage. By year 7, when *Behavioral Addictions: A New Solution to Very Old Problems* was written, these possibilities were starting to firm up: a *range* of Emotions had been encountered displaying the signature of Triggering. The relevance of the Self-Pact, at the time of writing the book you're now holding (year 11½), to the whole question of the pervasiveness of Triggering as it can manifest throughout the Emotional spectrum, has been arrived at "beyond a reasonable doubt."

Unfolding developments with the Self-Pact: Pathways of inner voyaging

As PERHAPS IS BECOMING CLEAR, the Energy of personal torments—The ENERGY!!—now available to carry us inwards, has work to do. An inner adventure, primarily, on many levels, experiential, leading to dimensions of awareness and comprehension—of *experiential knowing*—are now open to us to access.

The overall heading under which all such experiences—inner journeys—are subsumed could be described (if one is so inclined) as getting in touch with, or coming in contact with, "original causes and conditions." In other words, via various channels that become activated through the Energy of torments, realities are re-encountered in ways that are highly *immersive* and *experiential.* Such encounters place us in contact—in correspondence—with the cascading resonance of the Energy of Emotional torments—the ENERGY!!—from its preconscious origins on through developmental episodes of infancy, toddlerhood, early childhood, pre-teen, teenager, young adult, adult, midlife, and (in some of us for whom the Self-Pact is inaugurated much later in life) advanced middle age and early elderhood.

Wow.

What channels can the Energies of Emotional torments—the ENERGIES!!—traveling inwards, have at their disposal to reach us with their "messages?"

There are many. Bear in mind that every Self-Pact journey is, at least in part, a "Resonant" experience. Think of a tuning fork's being struck alongside a second tuning fork of the same pitch that has *not* been struck. Soundwaves from the struck-intoned tuning fork will travel (propagate) outwards from it, and the effect of "Resonance"—the waves encountering the second tuning fork—will induce an audible—and quite possibly visible—vibration (equal in pitch, and near equal in volume) in the non-mechanically-struck tuning fork. The dynamic of Resonance—

the waves from mechanically struck tuning fork being of the same pitch as the unstruck second tuning fork—"induces" the movement in the second tuning fork, resulting in both motion and sound emanating from the second tuning fork.

"Emotional Resonance" acts the same way. The Energies of torment—the ENERGIES!!—in the form of their Emotional charges will, when inner directed, send their waves forth into "interior space." Whatever past situations, encounters or events are encoded in memory—those including other people, places, things, situations, circumstances, conditions, institutions, ambitions, ideas, beliefs, expectations, disappointments and losses, etc.—which carry *any* Emotional hue (Resonance) similar to the emotional valence of torment-generated Energies—the ENERGIES!!—now detonated and propagating on the inner plane—will be restimulated—will seek to "vibrate" with an Emotional "tenor" and Resonance and, sometimes, . . . "recollections."

There are two ways we can speak of this process. The first (as earlier suggested) can be expressed as "channels" through which the "wavelengths," or Resonances of the Energies—the ENERGIES!!—are both transmitted and—if kindred Resonances are there to be activated on the "inside" (as is almost always the case)—through which the responding/corresponding Resonances also can make themselves known. These channels include each and all of the sensory faculties—visual, auditory, olfactory, taste, kinesthetic, proprioceptive, physical sensations/touch, and intuition. The Energies of torment—the ENERGIES!!—may find corresponding Resonances in any one or more of these areas that link either to particular, specific, preceding occurrences, or to some more general gestalt or pervasive milieu or pervasive theme (perhaps in the manner of a watercolor wash forming the background and surrounds of a more detailed painting)—taking more the form of an *environment* with its overall, attendant broad-brush Resonances being activated.

In the case of environmental or milieu resonances, what gets stirred up are not necessarily particular or specific events per se, but more the sense of an *ambience* that was chronic, and which constituted a backdrop, or setting, for much of what transpired over some life-epochs, or mini-epochs, of the tormented person's personal history.

"Resonance," in any such examples, may find its counterpoint in one specific sensory channel, or in an orchestration of two or more sensory channels.

With growing proficiency in Self-Pact activation when Triggered (part of the "deal" one makes with oneself), such inward travels—riding torments-based Energies—the ENERGIES!!—inwards, can unfurl rapidly.

In addition to the stimulation into activation, via Resonance, of individual sensory channels of perception, there are also more delayed effects stemming from the activation of torments-based Energy that is moving inwards.

The very fact that this ENERGY!!, far from being exorcised or otherwise peremptorily dismissed as "unacceptable" or "inadmissible" (good luck to you if you try that!), is not only expected (via Triggering), but *accepted* into the mix of our life experience, day in and day out, suggests that, when activated, it has more time to do its work—to search for, leaven up, and put us in touch with, those other Resonances that await. In other words, on the inner plane the Self-Pact permits this ENERGY!! to be loosed into the psyche, where it propagates to do what it needs to do—without being under constraints to be "done" in a more time-limited, episodic fashion.[27]

---

27. One way of comprehending this is that, for the first time in its embodied existence, the ENERGY!! itself has an actual witness to what *IT's* reality has been over long stretches of time. That witness is YOU (in the form of ego consciousness—your apparent personhood). Your bearing witness, during these inner excursions (as conducted by the Energy itself) to the Energy's own reality of torments, may be one of the rationales for the Energy to be so cooperative in this process of "self-exploration and discovery." Both sides gain something precious from this collaboration.

Hence, there are ambient, residual effects of this ENERGY!! being "loosed" within. The first of these (the order of mention of these effects is arbitrary) is our dream life. The Self-Pact seems to have an awakening effect on dreaming and, within dreams there exist innumerable Resonances that can stir and make their presence known. But this awakening to dreams and the resonances within dreams is not arbitrary. It is meaningful, for dreams are capable of conveying multi-dimensional linkages that relate, Energetically, to what has become a chronic problem of self-bedevilment: our array of torment-Triggered Energies. There are whole mindscapes and dreamscapes awaiting manifestation in service of helping us gain a greater, deeper comprehension of "original causes and conditions."

In addition to our dream life, there is an awakening of "hunches" and "intuitions" that can come to us during our wakeful hours. These awarenesses, inner promptings and inner knowings, though fueled by inwardly traveling torment-spawned Energies—ENERGIES!!—*are not themselves Triggering. They are, rather, enriching.* One can have surprisingly peaceful feelings and Emotions—not stemming from whatever immediate, intense awakenings one is having regarding any specific recollection of a past event or milieu (as would typically attach from consciously riding the Energy of torments inwards during a Triggering episode)—but, rather, from *the capacity, now being made manifest, of an ability to encounter, observe, acknowledge, and accept such Resonances, and the awarenesses that flow from them, **in a non-Triggered fashion.*** There is even a pleasure to be had in discovering this experience, paradoxically fueled by the Energy of torment itself.

Following the path onwards

In the prior passage the notion of "Resonance" receives frequent mention. Resonance is a ubiquitous quality; the vibrations which define it channel to us, in one form or another, almost all the entirety of our perceived experiences in our everyday lives.

However, "Resonance," in addition to being a pervasive, prosaic quality, possesses, as well, a unique ability. *"Resonance" has the capability of bridging across different dimensional domains.* It can calibrate itself to move seamlessly from one dimension of being (or non-being) to another—and back again; it can breach barriers that act as partitions to all of the senses, including those attributed to the physical world, and those considered to be the domain of the mental, or non-physical realms. Resonance can pass through the veil of the "mental" to inform the "spiritual," and vice-versa. It can provide a bridge between "words," and "the wordless." It can inform us of realms of prior happenings in our lives (past lives, too?), and challenge us to learn about "things" which, at the time of occurrence, we were not capable of "knowing," lacking, back then, mental faculties that we only developed later in our earthbound sojourn.

Resonance, as well, is not hampered by limitations of time. It operates (as is also true of our Emotions and Emotional life) in a realm that does not recognize the passage of time. There is only "Emotion" (E-Motion = Energy-in-Motion) Resonating—propagating through what we experience as past, present and future. But for Resonance, past, present and future are an amalgamated, single event. In other words, Resonance can translate between time and the timeless.

It is this pathway to *knowing*—to gaining experiential knowledge—that starts to expand the dimensions of what we come to know in following the Self-Pact. Answers to questions we, at an earlier time, didn't even know how to ask, await us there. New vistas are primed for our arrival—our "readiness to know."

In my own experiences of "following the path" of the Self-Pact, I gradually came to understandings of aspects of my background and formative years that gave me the assist I needed to live my life—though still with frequent Triggerings (as expected)—in a manner in which I became safe to be around, capable of loving, and, maybe even more impressive, *capable of tolerating being loved*, without having to cycle into destroying it all.

From where I come from, that's not "small change"; rather, that's a big, big, deal. The challenges I had faced, in entering into the Self-Pact, had been numerous and ongoing (as foreseen), but my progress, though dramatic in the beginning—minimizing the unleashing of damaging behavior on the outer world—had, over time, settled into a slower aggregation of multi-dimensional jigsaw puzzle pieces that continued to show up, and occasionally assemble as small features of a much larger tapestry. In other words, once I had settled in with the Self-Pact and experienced the benefits of the (relatively quick) "outer world" cessation of my victimizing those around me, my progress, thereafter, primarily had to do with inner travels and related discoveries, as I settled into a degree of progress that was slow, but definite.

IN MY BOOK *Behavioral Addictions: A New Solution to Very Old Problems*, written in 2015–2016, a question arose during the writing. This question was: In recovery from addiction(s), how healed is it possible to become? I devoted two chapters to this "healing" conundrum. The book itself was not expressly focused on Triggering or the Self-Pact (although those topics were not unrelated to the matter then at hand, and did receive a couple of mentions there). The focus was more on the generic qualities of "Addiction Energy"—having so many troublesome characteristics (what Freud would likely have dubbed as "perverse"), and pondering on what level, given their stubbornness and persistence, could they be reached, and healing be realized.

Here are the opening paragraphs to the relevant chapter:[28]

---

28. "Concerning One's 'Ultimate' Relationship with Addiction Energy: In Recovery, How Healed Is It Possible to Become?" Chapter 10 in *Behavioral Addictions: A New Solution to Very Old Problems*, (2016, Four Rivers Press, page 116.)

It is time to return to the topic of Addiction Energy—the *ENERGY!!*. We've been on quite an excursion, seemingly venturing far away from it. From presenting some case vignettes demonstrating how Behavioral Addictions can precede, coincide with, or develop subsequent to substance-based addictions; then on to considerations around self- and clinical diagnosis and treatment of Behavioral Addictions, including the unfolding of subsequent "surrenders"; and, finally, reframing recovery as a series of adventures in self-discovery rather than promises of assured outcomes, relatively few specific mentions, through these later chapters, have been made, along the way, of "Addiction Energy."

So now it's time to take this topic up again . . . for it has never really left us.

And, from what appears to be the case, Addiction Energy—the *ENERGY!!*—in all its displaceable glory, *doesn't* leave us. It seems as if its presence remains a "given," regardless of one's length of recovery, ferventness of devotion to recovery, and all attempts, no matter how well-grounded they may seem and how thoroughly regaled they are with earnest yearnings and honest efforts, to be rid, or free, of it.

This is difficult, indeed, to reconcile. In our world of linear thinking and rational sensemaking, honest efforts should be met with honest rewards. If we're "doing God's work," we should be divinely protected and "delivered from evil." If we're of noble character and possessed of utopian visions, focused efforts should be sufficient to bring them into manifestation. It just ain't fair that "it ain't necessarily so!!"[29]

The question that arises is: If Addiction Energy—the *ENERGY!!*—remains in the mix of who we are and what comprises us, where does that ultimately leave us?

---

29. . . . with apologies to, and heartfelt appreciation for, George Gershwin.

> Indeed, under such circumstances what does "healing"
> even mean? This is a riddle that evades facile resolution.

The forms of healing, 13 possibilities of which are elucidated in *Behavioral Addictions,* are all variations on adapting to certain conditions such as Triggering, and bouts of craving, and a batch of others—all of which are lifelong realites that have to be addressed via constant vigilance—recognizing that we exist in a state of remission rather than cure, requiring us to exert applied efforts on a daily basis to be aware of our vulnerability(ies)—*all* stemming from the realization that, at least in addiction terms, one never "has it made."

This level of "healing" could be termed "accommodative recovery." That anybody bedeviled with addictions in any area of behavior can get this far—ceasing destructive patterns of indulgence that have "committing suicide on the daily installment program" written all over them—that anybody can "wake up and smell the coffee," hit bottom and then surrender, withstand the rigors of going through withdrawal, endure the pain of "going sane," continue on to build a life that is demonstrably, on balance, being lived in furtherance of "goodness"—and see it all as worthwhile, despite constant challenges and enticing opportunities to "step off the world" and escape (a.k.a. relapse), yet . . . come what may, elect to stay the course through to the end—is an accomplishment that is so profound, private, and usually unsung—an accomplishment that is simply beyond the possibility of verbal language to describe or encompass.

Though not unique (there are many, many, many others besides me who have known from the beginning that "I'm in this for the long haul," and have lived it out that way), this has been my path—at least thus far.

However . . . my soul is a restless one. It was a few years ago (as of this writing) that I began, once again, to wonder, borrowing from the lyrics of jazz singer Peggy Lee's haunting rendition of the song "Is That All There Is?"[30] if, indeed, this level of healing: "accommodative recovery" is, "all there is."

What started to bring the question into the foreground is that—with nearly 50 years of sobriety (as I write this, less than two weeks to go) in terms of active alcoholism, 44 years of sobriety/abstinence from engaging in "bottom line" behavior in term of sex and 'love' addiction, and 11½ years into the Self-Pact—with all the blessings of a saved marriage and a loving spouse, along with a rich and love-filled family life—I have become aware that, while my ruinous, former behaviors of thoroughly indulging in addictions have changed profoundly, *my "tendencies" which, minus constant vigilance would likely have me "jumping the rails" without prior notice, **have not changed one iota**.* Despite all my sustained, daily efforts on a long-term basis, I have no immunity. I have dared to wonder about this; I have dared to ask myself "Why not?" Why, at this point, are "obsession" and "compulsion," along with the ever present possibility of succumbing to shock-wave based cravings, fantasies, seduction, along with their associated amnesia, still making themselves felt in worrisome ways? Upon reflection, it seems that my sobriety and what passes for recovery (in addiction terms), over all these years, has come about, and been sustained, *despite **not** being healed—or **not**, beyond a certain point, **being able** to be healed— rather than because I am healed.*

Was Peggy Lee, in that incomparable expression of ennui, disappointment and dysthymia in "Is That All There Is?" right? . . . Or is there some part of the picture I just haven't been getting, because I haven't yet become capable of recognizing it?

So the part of me that is very much in Job's camp has come out. But . . . I'm not knowingly (to me) entertaining any intentions to relapse into any of my destructive, addictions-riddled syndromes—which doesn't guarantee I won't, for no such guar-

---

30. URL for Peggy Lee's remarkable performance of *"Is That All There Is?"* https://www.youtube.com/watch?v=Fpg1UyEj7rI

antee exists, along these lines, in "addiction world." Win, lose, or draw, my commitment, even if "Is That All There Is?" turns out to be true, is still to "go the distance," regardless—as sober and aware a person as I can be. In other words, as far as I know, my commitment is still intact, and doesn't appear to be crumbling (though you, my reader, could always come to the conclusion that even bringing up a topic such as "Is That All There Is?" is evidential of a stewing disposition that could, sooner of later, take me out. That, of course, is always a possibility. I would never fault you for thinking that way about me).

But . . . back to Job of the Hebrew Bible: He raised his own questions, and objections. His situation was more severe than mine by many a country mile. Yahweh, that stern Hebrew God of the Old Testament, was not treating Job kindly. Deaths of his beloved others, including his wife and children, pestilence that inflicted great hardship on him—health challenges that were unremitting and not of his own making—all this was visited upon him by the God of his understanding, and . . . Job perse-vered . . . all the while, with each indignity, getting progressively more and more pissed off. He expressed his dismay in no uncer-tain terms about being so mistreated by his God. Using vernacular language, one might say that Job, pretty much at the end of his rope, verbally "ripped Yahweh a new one." Job's friends and associates were very conformist in their conservative, religious view of Yahweh, and not at all helpful. They told Job that he, Job, must have been screwing up something fierce, otherwise Yahew would not be treating him in such a punitive (or, as Job experienced it: such tawdry, and shabby) fashion.

But . . . Job had always been scrupulous in his observances, and *he knew it.* And . . . *he could not be dishonest with himself—with his own being—by denying this truth.* No shy violet, he kvetched and kvetched and kvetched—*holding to his core truth.* And . . . as the story goes, Yahweh finally granted him an audience, the sum and substance of which was: Yahweh bul-lied him. Swiss psychiatrist Carl Gustav Jung was fascinated and intrigued by the Job story. He took on the task of analyzing the encounter of Job and Yahweh from a psychological viewpoint. Jung's analysis of the encounter, as published in his monograph "Answer to Job," concluded that this remarkable confrontation between Yahweh and Job exposed Yahweh as the bully, stating that . . . it was Job, in his authentic righteousness, who showed Yahweh up as the abusive bully he was, and ultimately shamed him.[31]

The God I pray to is not Yahweh. (I typically pray to a dual, combined entity that roughly boils down to "'Loving Presence' and 'Unfathomable Mystery.'") But I figured that if thorough unhappiness based on unfair, unconscionable treatment by Job's god Yahweh could get "squared off" by such an encounter, then perhaps my own curiosity and undercurrents about "Is That All There Is?"—a.k.a. *Why Am I Not (More) Healed???*—if I made something of an inquiry about this, following the Emotions of dismay via "reaching inwards"—my Self-Pact commitment—in search of a higher truth, then, perhaps, I could be graced with a heavenly assist in coming to a comprehension about these matters.

Over the six-month span that followed, that is what transpired.

Heading towards Liberation and Freedom

It is at this point that I must emphasize to my dear readers that what I am about to share, stemming from my proceeding with "inner travels"—always precipitated by Triggering, instantly defaulting to the Self-Pact, then going forward with "inner travels"—are some of the fruits of these explorations, especially

---

31. "Answer to Job," final essay (p. 519) in *The Portable Jung* (Viking Press, New York, NY: 1971)

some of the more recent ones. *I wish to emphasize that I am not out to prove anything to anybody about the veracity of what I share. Perhaps*—at the level of "How true is this?"—*it's enough to say that this is, at least, one example of the kinds of "experiential knowing" the Self-Pact can lead to for those who, starting with the imperative to use it due to Emotionally-rowdy torments, continue to stick with it—first as an antidote to relapsing into the destructiveness of ongoing recurrences of Emotion-laden Triggerings, and then . . . as an adventure in its own right, as the discovery becomes increasingly in focus that the Energy has more to impart.*

The products of inner searching, and the yield that comes out of such a quest through immersive experiences, are highly personal and not provable through any recognized method of quantification. The sense of holding "truth"—beyond the revealing of literal truth in the form of specific recollections, chronological memories or perceptual awarenesses—*is an outworking of less-specific Energies in these deeper searches.* What the Energies present is a product of their *Resonances* that are capable of crossing dimensions, transcending space and time, conferring their own sense of "narrative truth" (perhaps in forms akin to "fable truth," "parable truth," "allegorical truth," "metaphorical truth," "trope truth," "legend truth," "metaphysical truth," "mythic truth," "synchronicitous truth"—maybe even "mystical truth"?), rather than distorting the knowledge they contain by trying to compress it in the form of delivering a "literal truth." From the standpoint of the larger horizons to which timeless Energies and Resonances have entrée (horizons beyond which may reside the very source of these Resonances), the task of addressing inquiries—for these Energies to fashion a suitable response to these inquiries—places a very difficult challenge before them. They are called upon to make translations out of the multiple-dimensional realities they sample, converting, as best they can, these ineffable sources and their "products" into "displays" or "presentations" of what can be comprehended by those of us having our current existence in four-dimensional space-time.

This is quite a burden for "Resonances" to accomplish! Reiterating the above, what they produce, as they attempt—in the process of criss/crossing the divides, to transpose, what is "across the divide" (and relevant to our inquiry) into comprehensible four-dimensional space-time representations and renderings—may be allegorical, artistic, creative, fantasy-appearing, symbolic, mystical, metaphorical, visual, auditory, olfactory, touch-oriented, coincidental, humorous (sometimes), synchronicitous, and on and on. *All such representations should be seen, and honored, as **that** which eludes specific, everyday appearance in our space-time world. Rather, they should be taken as efforts by these Energies to calibrate what they have to offer in a manner that can be **represented to**, and **comprehended by**, those of us (all of us!) who live in a space-time world.*

So here is what I have learned about me, with apologies as to the limitations I encounter in trying to convey any of this into formal verbal language.

The first thing I would mention is that, as the use of the Self-Pact—born of necessity, and continued to be resorted to in default fashion to constructively engage ongoing Triggerings—starts to turn up the volume (on the inside) of surfacing, Emotion-laden torments: Emotions, memories, awarenesses, inner encounters, re-lived anecdotes, a fine granularity of moving images, impressions, "still" (frozen) images (very specific and detailed), swaths of brief (yet specific) moving images, sounds, tastes, visual phenomena, auditory phenomena, body/touch-related surfacings, Emotional upwellings, crystallizing awarenesses, etc., etc.—*some combinations of these components start to show up, as longer, more extended, immersive experiences.* (All of this is consistent with the use of the Self-Pact becoming more commonplace and practiced.)

These are all pieces of a puzzle, yet to be fully collated and assembled, but generally orbiting around the principle of "original causes and conditions."

Making such connections between an Emotional torment

and "something on the inside" that bears strong relevance in the form of some detail or other can be a very exciting experience. The pain of suffering, the cause of which is usually (habitually!) attributed to outer world provocations and circumstances, is, even in a tiny way, revealed to have a strong nodal point of correspondence (or, if you will, *Resonance*) on the "inside." This is not new. Resonances are the surviving relics of past history—including the deep past. Such relics may be new to awareness, but they are very old as to how long, in the course of a life, they have been active, and in some sense "ruling the roost."

So the plot thickens. Assemblage of puzzle pieces bearing the fine detail of scrimshaw and fillegrie start to flesh out a personal history, which is increasingly recognizable as such. These puzzle pieces carry convincing "fingerprints"—print-marks—of early events that, for whatever reason, have had an imprinting impact on me (maybe you, also, have some of these?). They "spin," to the extent that memory (as we think of it) can convey some sense of tangible reality to the events they signify; traumatic antecedents of early-childhood, including experiences of terror (possibly from numerous sources) may collate the Emotional experience of terror—of being terrified—with specific events that account for these experiences of terror, melding these two modes of experiencing/knowing: the Emotional repercussions of such events and the specific recollections of what events launched them. *In a moment like this, the "Emotion" and the cognition/cerebral form of knowing, are conjoined into a moment of "sure knowledge."* The Energy—one dollop of it, anyway—of Emotional torment has been returned to, visitied, and rejoined with, its source: the conditions that split it off and created it. The Energy has made contact with "an original cause and condition." This is healing for the Energy, and liberating for the person for whom a tiny, yet definite, bit of mystery—a previously unknown but now known bit of history, has now been laid bare, and resolved.

In my own experiences with the Self-Pact, much of the earlier years of engaging with it consisted, increasingly over time, of these kinds of encounters and cognitive awakenings. The outer world of my immediate family was much safer in terms of my "reactive temperament," and I was getting tastes of what it means to achieve a sense of—moments of—reconciliation of, and with, my multidimensional self on the "inside."

The whole thing, on balance, was very successful, highlighted by increasing my proficiency with—though not decreasing my need for—the Self-Pact.

It's fair to say that, over time, most of the grist and sawdust of my very difficult childhood was, via the Self-Pact, accessed, and congealed, to a point of recognizing, within the bounds of conscious memory (which probably, in my case, kicked in during my second year of embodied life), the highly likely milieu in which I got pretty soundly bashed, and *imprinted*: an alcoholic, violent, tyrannical father; a mother who was a classic enabler—in way over her head, who appeased my father and could not protect my brothers and me from him; two brothers: one older, who hated me as he himself was hated by our father; a younger brother who was a bit of a family mascot, diverting attention away from what was both real and ugly in that family. Outcomes: father: got sober at age 48 picking potatoes out of the fields at Bridgewater State Hospital in Massachusetts. He put together 15 years of sobriety (it was a renaissance for him), then relapsed and never made it back. He died at age 66 of lung cancer); mother: she formed an unholy collusion with both my older and younger brothers, who badgered her ceaselessly for special favors; older brother: he became an emotional cripple who "retired" by age 40 due to his being placed on permanent medical leave by the Fortune 500 company he worked for; younger brother: smartest of the three of us, he became (eventually) an anesthesiologist—a great occupation for a drug addict to hide out in. He couldn't sustain his career while being pursued by his cocaine dealer for back-payments of his cocaine debts, so he "went underground." Eventually, after living with our elderly mother for several years during which she (once again) was a classic enabler of his drug habits, he "went underground" for keeps, killing himself via an irreversible drug cocktail he had cooked up.

It's curious to note that although the factual outlines of some of what I have just mentioned were known to me prior to using the Sef-Pact, they existed in my then-conscious memory as simple, episodic anecdotes and at-a-distance events that really didn't string together in a connected way as part of the "milieu" of my childhood. It was through the Self-Pact that these puzzle pieces, along with many, many others, of discrete memories started to assemble as a cohesive scenario—as a whole-cloth narrative.

That's probably about as much of my childhood and "family-of-origin" situation as you need to know. I won't, for the sake of doing so, go out of my way to dwell on any further specific aspects, personnages or galloping pathology (the rest of it got worse in a big hurry) any further. That's been done elsewhere, and, having hoed those fields pretty thoroughly, I have no further need to do so here.

So . . . several years of continuing, on a daily basis, to honor my commitment to the Self-Pact—my pact with me—I had enough of the picture to know, with a high degree of probability—as admixtured by numerous collisions of Emotional torments and specific cognitive awakenings—of where I had been—and something of what had happened to me, and what had been *done* to me. The pathology, all around, was pretty damn deep. (To put it mildly, the clinical, minimalistic, euphemistic-oh-so-polite expression used to describe me was: "You are *'disturbed.'"* There's a descriptive, if calculated to be "not too disturbing," diagnosis for you!!)

With these increasing bits of visiting my past, either by "going back in time" to experience them, or being in *certain frames of mind* (via the Self-Pact) *that gave these deeper aspects of my formative history the opportunity and the means to "come forward in time" from their frozen, imprisoned existences in that ancient past—to a point where they could, with intention combined with my welcoming acceptance,* **meet me in my present reality—** *expanding my own experience of the present; being fully absorbed by both Emotional and situational antecedents of my whole consequential life—I continued to gain in self-knowledge.*

I also suspect that, over this span of time, I harbored a wish—maybe implicitly a demand to the Heavens—that when enough of these kinds of deep immersion journeys, of Emotional torments and cognitive/"mental" awakenings of actual historical antecedents had been digested—I might "heal" to the point of being, no longer, in any way, living at the mercy of a Triggering neurology.

THE PLOT WAS ABOUT TO THICKEN some more. Having already begun to feel, as I have earlier expressed, a sense of frustration—maybe even defeat—that despite my remarkably redeemed life—with so much to show for it in terms of sobriety(ies), my love-filled marriage, my family life, along with other activities related to vocations and avocations—it was increasingly galling (as I have previously mentioned) to recognize that I was still among the afflicted. Despite all of the above, along with my own mighty efforts, as spiced with Utopian fantasies, *I was not healed*—at least in the manner and to the extent that I thought *might* happen . . . and also thought I thoroughly deserved.

This was the quandary that I was stuck with for many months. My Jobian self was raising objection to my plight, and I was seeking "an audience" with "to Whom it may concern." I now knew about my personal history, but . . . despite knowing the contours of my history, I realized that I was missing some octaves in my makeup.

And then it came to me, right out of a Self-Pact-inspired dream. The short form is this: The revelation suddenly burst upon the scene, under the heading: ***"The CLASH!!!"*** From my dream log, a quite-verbatim translation: "My psyche split under the clash of irreconcilable Emotions: Love/Hate, Hope/Despair, Fantasy/Fear, Security/Terror, et al."

Here's another subsequent dream note (about a week later): "The act of Triggering confirms the existence of a psychical split—a 'split psyche.'"

Two days later, a Self-Pact Resonance, boiled down into language, continued: "Triggering is the reenactment of the original Clash of Irreconcilable Emotions. Triggering carries with it echoes of the Resonances of 'original causes and conditions,' in which the time dimension collapses/collapsed as a function of the onslaught of the original clashes. These polarities create the tensions of existence—along with the 'time' dimension."

What a sudden bombardment of annunciations—the first salvo of proffered responses to my existential dilemma! These Resonance-based utterances gave me a lot to think about over the following weeks. Things were happening; another piece of the puzzle had surfaced. More previously missing pieces of the puzzle were soon to be unfurled.

About three weeks following the inaugural salvo, new information commenced to surface. "When splinters come calling," followed two days later by another dropped shoe: ". . . whatever Clashes of Irreconcilable Emotions and simultaneous fracturing occurred to my inchoate self/soul . . . 'I,' *Stephen Rich Merriman, am one of the resulting **splinters** of such events* and, in the absence of awareness of them, I have been, unbeknownst to me, completely driven, directed and run by them . . . ."

So here were two distinct hints to follow. *First,* "I," the Energy that comprises me, had primordial roots existing within what the Resonance (however clumsily translated) designated as "Inchoate Wholeness." And *Second,* my primordial ordeal of not just "having" splits (an awareness that was not new to me at all as a result of all the work I had done via the Self-Pact over a number of years, in which I had become objectively acquainted with my "split," "Triggering" nature that had been on parade my whole life)—but . . . *being* a "*split*" . . . *being, myself, a splinter—a shard—was, finally, revealed to me, and the truth it held was instantly recognizable and identifiable to me.*

This information bumped up my awareness a considerable notch. The fact that I am not simply a person with "splits" in his makeup but, additionally, *my whole personhood—who I am; how I was created from an environment of "Emotional Clashes"—is itself a splinter—was/is, for me, a game changer. Recapping: I am not merely a person with splintered parts; I am, myself, such as I am, a splinter, a shard.*

This sure as hell gave me something to think about, with Emotions not far behind.

Several days following the latest "information dump," I wrote in my dream/Self-Pact Log : " . . . Rage at *being* a splinter, rather than only (feeling) 'rage at *having* splits.'"

There was so much in this new information—again, the product of immersive experiences, rather than just intellectual head-scratching (as if pondering and surmising from a safe distance). I didn't know where things were headed, but I had the feeling—and sensation—that things were moving—were going somewhere.

The whole notion of "the Clash of Irreconcilable Emotions" carried a tremendous degree/amount of Resonance to it. I felt motivated to make a casual list of the anything-but-casual clashes that might be of sufficient intensity to create these splits—to have created "me" (one or more of the splinters of such an event). Some of these entries might carry enough conflicting Energy to do the job: destroying "Inchoate Wholeness." Others, with their own collisions of Irreconcilable Emotions, might not, of themselves, be powerful enough to do it—but . . . they would certainly react to the presence of fractured Energies of those events that *are* powerful enough to create the major splits.

NOTE: Concerning the list of "Irreconcilable Emotions"

In the list that follows, don't think of various, paired terms in the manner of their more formal dictionary definitions. Rather, think of them as Emotional valences—*each paired term harboring a point of Emotional valence—generating its own heat.*

For any of the paired terms—taken individually as dyadic entries—see if you can (yes!) imagine, maybe even detect—for each entry, what the dueling, mutually inimical Energies would feel like as they clash, tearing away at the fabric of "Inchoate Wholeness." See if you can gain a sense of this. If you're really brave (no additional points for bravery), see if you can imagine what "Inchoate Wholeness" feels like as it is suddenly riven apart by (quite possibly) its own awakening, conflictual innards.

Here are the dyadic pairings:

Clashes of Irreconcilable Emotional Energies:
Dyadic Candidates

'love'[32]/hate   safety/perdition

---

32. Please note: The word Love is displayed here as 'Love' because most human experiences of love—including, but not limited to, romantic love—consist of minimal presence of unconditional, 'pure' *love,* and an overabundance of "conditional love" in which love is compromised, or corrupted, by being front-loaded with mind-numbing attraction/distraction, expectations, implicit and/or explicit demands, obsessions, neediness and endless projections and manipulations—all of which can give rise to shock-wave disillusionments that generate the heat for the "clashes" that follow. Unfettered, unconditional love is real, and profoundly beautiful to experience and witness, . . . but it is rare. "Clashing" would *not* be part of its MO (modus operandi). For a sublime exposition of the process in which "polluted love" (my term) can transfigure, interpersonally, into unconditional love, I highly recommend John A. Desteian's

exuberance/dysphoria

hope/despair

win/lose

gain/loss

trust/betrayal

faith/disillusionment

good/evil

kindness/cruelty

safety/peril

wellbeing/pain

'love'/indifference

sensing/numbness

in control/out of control

having it made/reversal of fortune

calm/panic

lust/abstinence

faithful/cheating

adored/despised

self-righteousness/guilt

expectation/disappointment

neediness/compassion

secure/at risk

peacefulness/harm

faith/abandonment

hidden/exposed

hunger for love/destruction of love

reliability/dereliction

powerful/powerless

gracious/selfish

taken seriously/disregarded

jubilation/deflation

security/destitution

self-sacrificing/selfish

on a path/rudderless

desire /rejection

craving/deprivation

yearning/futility

satiation/hunger

joy/depletion

peace/violence

conscience/instinct

refined/brutish

life/death

admiration/disgrace

male/female

prosperous/impoverished

rich/poor

peace/terror

flowing/blocked

free/enslaved

arousal/restraint

whole/split

comfort/anxiety

permanence/suddenness

secure/robbed

happiness/dysphoria

coping/out of control

complete/inadequate

secure/redundant

liked/hated

'loved'/needy

truthfulness/deception

noble/criminal

virtue/corruption

selflessness/exploitation

belief/hopelessness

being loved/abandonment

gentleness/violence

book *Coming Together—Coming Apart: The Play of Opposites in Love Relation-ships* (new edition: Chiron Publications, 2021).

water/phosphorus	exploitation/'love'
faithful/screwing around	perpetrator/victim
predatory/prey	giving/taking away
terror/relief	compassion/passion
heroism/cowardice	risk-taking/safety
building/destroying	enjoy/detest
secrecy/openness	escapism/reality
falling in 'love'/falling in hate	explosion/implosion
empathic/rapacious	moral/immoral
sentient/unfeeling	careful/reckless
reliable/delinquent	safe/dangerous
ideals/schemes	forthrightness/intrigue
acquiesce/revolt	superego/id
lies/truths	mercy/cruelty
nourishing/venomous	euphoria/misery

Note: These aforementioned dyadic pairings burst upon the scene in quick batches over several days.

The Crushing of "Inchoate Wholeness"

THESE DYADS RAISED CERTAIN ADDITIONAL questions of their own. The biggest one was: For each of the pairings, it's easy to see them as fostering states of ambivalence, rather than full-out clashes. Truly, I think most people—except those of us who are chronically Triggering-prone (with all our various *Emotional* torments)—experience their Emotions, as they engage with their day-to-day lives, as manifesting as back-and-forth swings of moods, along with accompanying mentations within them— as "ambivalent" (ambi-valent), and, quite often (depending on the Emotional admixture in play), as ambiguous.

However, for those of us who are Triggerers, it's a different story: we are caught in the "irreconcilable" part. For us, there is not much capacity to tolerate ambiguity, let alone ambivalence, and get on with our lives. Rather than "riding" ambivalence, for us it's almost always an immediate, intensity-driven "All or Nothing!!"

As I was pondering these stark differences in how "normal" people deal with the "irreconcilable," I realized that, for them, the *clash* rarely, if ever, happens. More attentiveness to this discrepancy between those (like me) who are Triggerers, and those who are not, yielded a small set of diagrams that helped me to comprehend the differences. These diagrams are depictions of a couple of different kinds of waveforms. They are a good analogue to the workings of raw Emotions, and offer insights into these Emotions, and, how the "Clashes of Irreconcilable Emotions" can arise within "Inchoate Wholeness," one of the mainsprings of what we, as Triggerers, have to contend with.

SO . . . here they are:

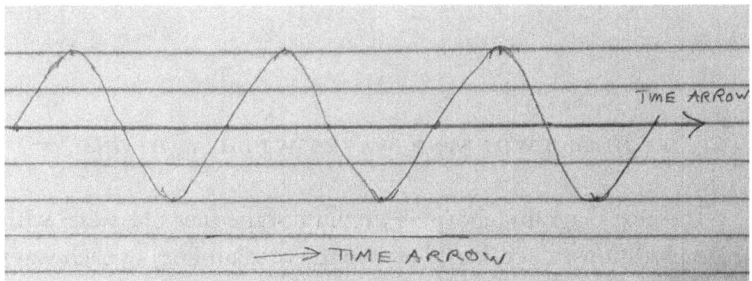

FIGURE ONE: SINE WAVES

The first diagram is a sine wave. If you were to hold a steady pitch via whistling or humming a single note, and that tone was fed into an oscilloscope, it would look pretty much like what this diagram looks like.

Every complete journey (in this diagram, proceeding from left to right), starting from the centrally located median line on up to the top, then "from up on down"—travelling from the top of the waveform—going down the slope, crossing the median

line, and continuing on the the very bottom of the wave form—
and then back up to the starting-point (the median line)—
colloquially: traveling from the median line up to the "peak" of
the wave (above the median line) down through the median line
to the bottom of the "trough" (below the median line), and then,
again, traveling back up from the trough, or bottom of the waveform, up to the the median line—is a rendering of one complete
cycle, or oscillation, of that tone. The oscillation (alternating
current/energy) moves both above and below the median line,
and . . . the very presence of oscillation means that this sequence
is occurring along a "timeline."

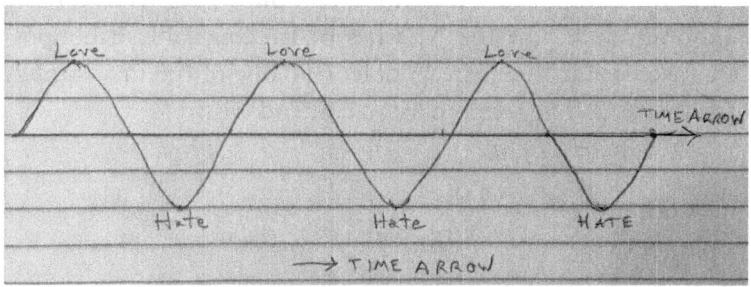

FIGURE TWO: SINE WAVES WITH ADD-ONS

The next diagram (above) is a replica of the first sine wave, with
major additions: Each "peak" (above the median line) of each wave
form is depicted as a "Love" extreme, and each "trough," or "bottom"
(below the median line) is depicted as an extreme of "Hate."

Bear in mind that (once again), the waves (we might call the
second diagram "Emotion waves") are also transpiring/mani-
festing along a "time- line" (as denoted by the median line). This,
in short, means that while the Emotions depicted—"Love" and
"Hate"—are arguably violently oppositional, they each manifest
in their own segment of the time dimension, and . . . their manifesta-
tions, for all intents and purposes, do not overlap. They co-exist, after
a fashion, but they do not bludgeon one another out of existence by
clashing. As a function of their coexisting, those people who can

experience ambiguity as a response to conflicting Emotions have the dynamic of "ambiguity," as just described, going for them. Bear in mind that life on the sign-wave crests and faults—crests into peaks and descents into troughs (and back again)—via lovely, relatively gentle gradations of slope (change), makes, over time, the divisions (and experiences) between the acute Emotion of "Love," and the acute Emotion of "Hate," rise and fall without getting in each other's way. The alternating back and forth between them both (along with their respective Emotional extremes) is profoundly buffered by the passage-of-time transitions, which smooth out the changes from one extreme Emotional state to the other (and back again).

The next diagram is of another alternating current pattern, as depicted on the oscilloscope. It's call a "square wave," and it looks like this:

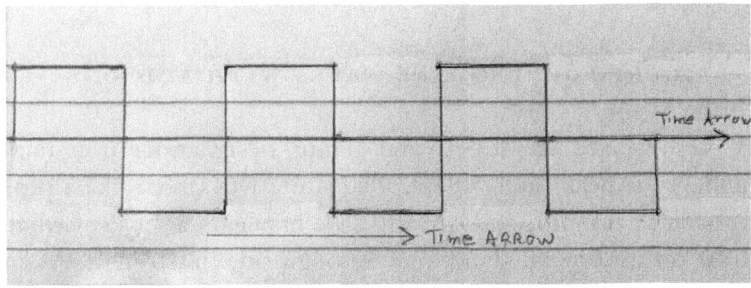

FIGURE THREE: SQUARE WAVES

The roots of this pattern are to be found in basic electrical engineering (where there is focus on designing square-wave circuits involving rectifying alternating current (AC) into direct current (DC), as part and parcel of various kinds of power supplies used to power a wide range of electronic equipment.

It is also the raw Energy pattern of a Triggerer.

Notice that, unlike the sine wave with its aesthetic, silky curves—a gentle hand-off from positive extremes to negative extremes, and back again ("Love" and "Hate" in the prior example)—

with square waves there is no polite buffering between these extremes. The "ride" from full Emotion "+" to full Emotion "-" and back again, is near-instantaneous—almost completely unbuffered. It's true that square waves (in fact, anything involving "waves," as we understand then), do proceed along a time continuum, but that fact does nothing to mitigate the relatively rough slams of moving peak-to-trough, and back again—and on and on and on . . . it goes.

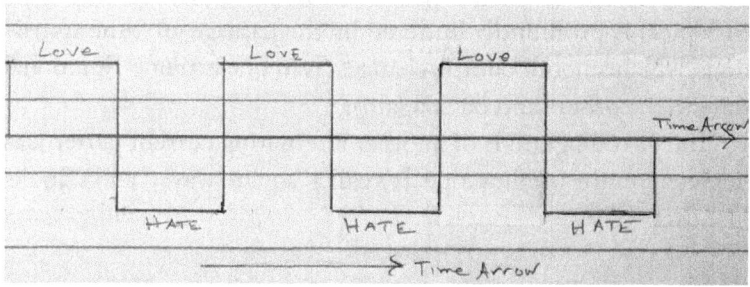

FIGURE FOUR: SQUARE WAVES WITH ADD-ONS

If we place the "Love" and "Hate" designations over (and under) the peaks and valleys of square waves (more like a procession of summits and canyons), we may gain a sense of what, from an Emotional standpoint, a rough ride this truly is. As an Emotional profile, reactivity is always amped up and, for most of those (of us) who are Triggerers and don't know the deeper dynamics that cause it, we are held hostage to it as it "runs us and ruins us."

So, in the example of the square wave, the time dimension, while still there, turns out to be a threadbare barrier between the extremes. It demarcates the territory of each extreme, but does almost nothing to buffer, and mitigate, the switch from one to another—and from "another" back to "one."

This extreme switching—switching from full on "+" to full on "-" in the flick of an eye (really the "flick of an Emotion")—is very, very wearing. In the electrical engineering world, power supplies that are based on square wave circuitry require beefed-up components—especially robust capacitors—to withstand the rapidity and fierceness of this kind of switching.

Using square waves as a model, note that the powerful, incompatible Emotions/Energies are immediately adjacent to each other, switching back and forth. But . . . although very close by one another, they are not (yet) overlapping or clashing.

In the human "psychological/neurological" sphere, Emotional rigidity: cultivated, strict, unyielding, impermeable—a kind of barrier—is the only way to (try to) survive/assuage this "back and forth" onslaught of these incompatible Energies. It may sort of work for a while to build some kind of psychical exoskeleton equivalent to keep on going . . . but it's a losing game.

Here's what happens (and it ain't pretty).

The square waves start to lose the integrity of separation-tasked partitioning. The boundaries begin to shift and inter-mingle. Here is a simplified schematic depiction of that:

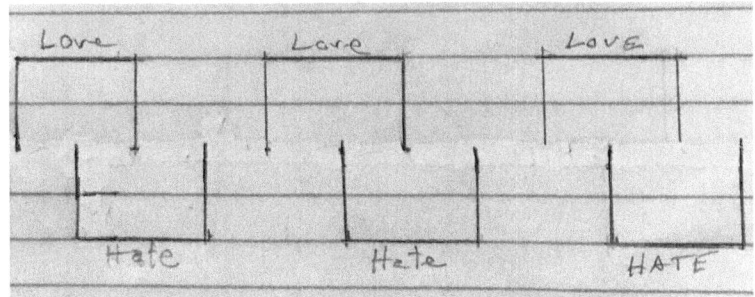

FIGURE FIVE: SQUARE WAVES WITH PARTITIONING
BOUNDARIES BECOMING UNSTABLE, LEADING TO
THE COLLAPSE OF SQUARE-WAVE PARTITIONINGS
—AND, ALONG WITH IT . . .
THE COLLAPSE OF THE TIME DIMENSION

Figure 5 schematicizes the breakdown of the partitions between "Love" and "Hate." Now, with the partitioning boundaries thoroughly perforated, the respective ENERGIES!! start to swirl around each other—with greater, ever-accelerating intensity.

What is also starting to happen, that is of even more importance—of "first-order" importance? It is this: The time dimension is collapsing between the two extremes. Here's a follow-up question: What happens when the time dimension suddenly collapses?

Here's what happens:

Without, any longer, any partition (as conferred by the time dimension) separating them, the "Clash of Irreconcilable Opposites" suddenly occurs in a timeless flash. The result (as represented pictorially) is this: (see Figure 6 and 7.)

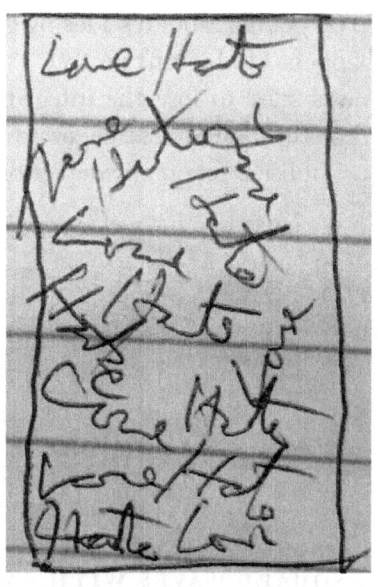

**FIGURE SIX: THE COLLAPSE OF
THE TIME BOUNDARY—THE CLASH
OF IRRECONCILABLE OPPOSITES**

Time (at least in the Emotional realm) is disintegrating.

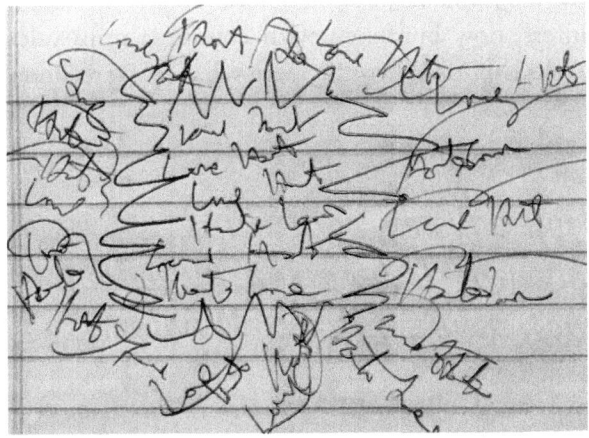

**FIGURE SEVEN: THE FINAL DENOUEMENT
THE DESTRUCTION OF INCHOATE WHOLENESS—
AS BROUGHT ON BY COLLAPSING BOUNDARIES
ALONG WITH THE TIME DIMENSION—THE "CLASH
OF IRRECONCILABLE EMOTIONAL ENERGIES"**

The above image is a representational portrayal of the amazing dynamics of all that's left of "Inchoate Wholeness" (our square-wave model has been the stand-in for this) following the "Clash between Irreconcilable Opposites" and the rupturing of partitioning boundaries, with the time dimension collapsing along with them.

What is left, and has left the scene, is the expulsion/dispersal/propagation of countless Emotional shards and splinters: EACH and ALL of which carry within them the valences of Irreconcilable Emotions—ALL of which are propagating multi-dimensionally, exploding and imploding at the same (lack of) time.

The shards—the splinters—of the previously coexisting "Wholes" of "'Love'" and "Hate" have been split asunder, flying off in all directions and dimensions as "Emotional Shrapnel." The original "Inchoate Wholeness" is shattered—beyond retrieval—beyond any chance to again coalesce and become an embodiment of potential wholeness as, in its origins, it was "once upon a time." They, the jagged edges of countless shards and splinters, now burdened with countless mini-valences of unresolvable Emotional conflict, are what they are, and it—the situation—is what it is.

My own odyssey, continued: Approaching Liberation, Freedom and (maybe), a new kind of Wholeness (?)

YOU MAY RECALL that what gave rise to this train of thought was a kind of combination of ennui and sadness (along with a bit of piss and vinegar) regarding the limited extent of my own healing (as you may remember, hauntingly Resonant with Peggy Lee's version of the song "Is That All There Is?").

I copped to allowing myself to acknowledge that there was a deep dissatisfaction within me which persisted, notwithstanding a dangerously destructive background littered with the detritus of alcoholism, other addictions, recklessly indulged cravings, and my growing sobriety in a number of these areas (as I write this I am now one day away from celebrating [if I make it] 50 years of continuous sobriety from active alcoholism). I looked at Job's struggle a bit, and felt somewhat emboldened to claim my discontent—*not* a complaint about the many blessings that I *have* received over these many years (they are undeniable), but . . . the fact that I am *still* afflicted with as much need for "sustained and personal exertion," and "constant vigilance" as I was in my long-ago situation as "newly sober," or "abstaining," or becoming "clean" in any of the areas of my addiction-riddled past.

So in my own, probably half-assed way—because, as a Triggerer, for the past 11½ years I was continuing to default to the Self-Pact on (of course, Triggering being what it is) a daily, recurring basis—I finally started to get around to raising my concerns about "me and healing" during those latter-day ongoing inner travels.

Over about a six-month period, gradually, but definitely, my plight was heard, and taken up within my psyche. It's even possible, as I see it, that the impetus to raise such questions (or exhibit such impudence—depending on how you look at it), was itself packaged for me by my Energies of torment in order to force me in some fashion to take on the quest.[33]

So here is how it all boils down *for me* regarding what the Self-Pact placed before me, that I might awaken further to a higher degree of comprehension regarding me, my origins, and my quest for "healing."

Bear in mind (one more time) that the assembled puzzle-piece narrative I shall present is nothing I am trying to prove to anyone regarding its veracity. You who are reading this book (if you've gotten this far), likely have your own discoveries to make, questions to ask, and resolutions to be sought out regarding *your* own life, identity, circumstances, maybe destiny—and, yes, *your own personal narrative—yet to be assembled.*

So *my narrative*, which has served to free me up from my earlier consternation, and has also led to my liberation and freedom from the tyranny of the dynamics of my previously unknown history, *is very satisfying to me.* There is nothing left to prove about it. "I," and the Energies that stir within me, are the only producers and consumers of it.

However, once again I wish to state that *what **may** hold true for you, is to take my narrative, along with the Self-Pact inner journeys that fashioned it, as being **indicative** of what, in fact, the Self-Pact actually **can** do—born first of necessity, and evolving, sequentially, into adventures of self-discovery, and then on to some form of deliverance.*

HERE IS MY NARRATIVE:

As I write this section, I wish to acknowledge that today,

---

33. Although I have been using the Self-Pact on a daily basis for over 11½ years, this whole book is a sum product of Self-Pact exploration and yieldings, going back only over the past 6 months or so—a *very* fertile time for fresh, cascading awarenesses, indeed! Of course, this "six-month yield" builds on the shoulders of those prior years.

January 30th, 2021, I mark 50 years of continuous sobriety from active alcoholism. At 3:35 A.M. on Saturday, January 30th, 1971, I was thrown out of the Club Casablanca in Harvard Square, Cambridge, Massachusetts for the last time. I was done. I'm only 3 months into writing the first draft of this book, and it seems a proper task that on the day of my sober anniversary which commenced a half-century ago, I am now setting forth to write this section on "Liberation and Freedom."

In accordance with my narrative, here, in general, is how it begins:

As far as we know—well, as far as "I" know—there is no discriminating, continuous, consistent rational faculty in the early days, months and first few years of our earthly lives. However, whatever form we are in during our early, earthly life is *highly impressionable*—very much at the mercy of whatever is occurring around it—around us—to us, from the outer world.

The "outer world," relatively speaking, is always surrounding us, regardless of our size and shape at any point and moment of our existence.

When "I" was a fetus, the walls of the womb were part of the external world surrounding me. When I was larger, and birthed, the outer world started just beyond the skin of an infant's growing body. Regardless of the state of the ability (or lack of ability) to "think," or "make sense of," there is, at all times, neurological *reactivity* (stimulus /response) to whatever is going on in the outer world, as a direct result of the body's neurology registering and absorbing whatever that may be.

Imprints and instant reactivity, at a certain pitch, lead to psychical splits, impressions and fragmentation, and (eventually) to stencils that become reactive overlays to our interactions/ encounters with external reality—*becoming instantaneous, default projections onto the "outer world"*—**our** *response* to what we *think* the "outer world" is serving up to us. This process, so automatic and (to us) so unconscious, provides us a profoundly false tableau for sense-making.

Now I'll boil this down, at least in part, reverting to the first person singular narrative.

The Energies that comprise me were all sourced in an Inchoate Wholeness. "I" was not "I," nor "me," in that primordial environment.

Those Energies that were to coalesce into "me"—give rise to my existence—were in their own harmonic swirl, presumably in balance, and "harmonizing with the spheres."

"*Something*" occurred which, Energetically, I know (though cannot prove) was a Clash of Irreconcilable Emotion-charged Energies. My narrative has not assembled to the point of knowing, or having a sure sense of, when, along a timeline, the clock stopped and this Clash occurred. But the Resonance that has informed me of this is very, very strong indeed.

I suppose that such a Clash could stem from the Big Bang of 13.7 billion years ago, as a moment when what was to become our whole Universe, in its infancy, was birthed out of a colossal, unimaginable detonation that burst through a "VOID," creating not just material matter and dark matter, but the *timeline* as well (hence, "four-dimensional space-time.")

Whatever caused that cataclysmic, convulsive detonation— maybe "creative destruction?"... or "destructive creation"?—was an event that not only birthed our Universe, *but created time itself.* Its imprints on our physical reality are there to be observed and listened to by any good radio-astronomy observatory. Point an antenna (a dish antenna) at any apparently less populated (by stars and galaxies) area of the visible cosmos, and, in the illusory "empty space," *there* are the footprints left by the Big Bang. Those footprints are called "The Cosmic Microwave Background."

Whether the shock-wave Resonances of the Big Bang are themselves responsible for setting off countless other Resonance-induced "Clashes of Irreconcilable Energies" is possible to con-template, but that's about as far as one can go with this. Nevertheless, the precedent of a mighty explosion emanating

from a "VOID" (the flip-side of an Inchoate wholeness??) creating (from our standpoint) the "all that is" cannot be entirely
dismissed as a template for the creation that has, astronomically,
followed: the Cosmos—and that includes *"me," and . . . "you."*

In my own history, the "fact" that Irreconcilable Energies—
Emotional in nature (<u>E</u>-<u>M</u>otion = <u>E</u>nergy in <u>M</u>otion)—
destroyed the Inchoate Wholeness housing the Energies that
were to coalesce as "me," is beyond question. Whether, in the
frame of a life-time, this destruction got Triggered by tendrils
stemming from original Big-Bang Resonances, or the Resonances
of karmic obligations still unmet, or whether it may have related
to intrauterine trauma of some sort in the process of fetal development and subsequent birth (I ventured out into the world
"three weeks post-due," *clearly <u>not eager</u> to "get on with it!!")*—or
perhaps getting Triggered off by "knock-down, drag-out" fights
between my parents, when surges of adrenalin would cross the
placenta, reaching "me," while still in the womb, to ill effect—or
whether it was ignited, post-birth, by being a terrified, frozen,
captive witness to my father's acts of sadism aimed particularly
at my older brother (my father's namesake), even as I, writhing
with hatred towards my father for his acts of cruelty—now
become a victim of my own self-hatred for being so profoundly
impotent to intervene and make the cruelty cease, with no possibility of unloading the Emotional toxins that were building
within me—or times when he would physical grab me and my
brothers and yank us, still fast asleep, out of our beds at 3 A.M.,
make us stand, naked, in military formation, terror-frozen like
statues as he barked German commands at us and forced us to
stand at attention, "COUNT-OFF!!" and "DRESS-RIGHT-
DRESS!!"—*any* combination of these (and other indignities I
haven't mentioned) could have set off the smashing of Inchoate
Wholeness as an unavoidable event in my formative (perhaps
better termed "deformative") history.

Any and/or all of these toxic influences—as repeated numerous
times and in various combinations and settings in that precon-

scious/lack of objective, non-analytical consciousness—with its reactive neurology—destroyed and smashed that comfort, solace, safety, inclusivity of those Energies which, less the clashes and chaos and violence, may have been capable of producing a more "cohesive" and "whole" person than I turned out to be.

As I was to discover in my Self-Pact inner travels, what the "Clashes of Irreconcilable Emotions" produced was not a whole person at all. Those clashes produced multidimensional splinterings of chards, propagating in all directions. All of those chards and splinters, as they were driven, projected, expelled—jettisoned—out and away from implosion/explosion of smashed Inchoate Wholeness—were laced with bits and pieces of "Irreconcilable Energies"—constantly grating and grinding against one another, in the process becoming the Emotional equivalent of Shrapnel. One (or perhaps some finite number) of those shards— those splinters—is "me." I am not a whole person. I may be a "person" who has splits—*but I am, myself, a splinter, a shard.* I lack octaves of what it takes to be "whole." *What takes Wholeness's place is . . . the multidimensional cacophony of Emotional Shrapnel.*

This is the response to my dogged question about "How healed can I become?" and, "What are the limits of my healing?"

The answer, straightforward and conclusive, is: I am not capable of fuller healing because I lack the "octaves" that make Wholeness—in the manner of matured, *"Choate'* Wholeness ," along with post-birth cohesiveness—possible. Therefore, in terms of what I envisioned healing and Wholeness to be, they are not available to me. The Wholeness of which "I," in the form of the Energies that comprise me, was a harmonious part, was smashed in the cauldron of Emotional Clashes. Shards and splinters— Emotional Shrapnel—the projectiles of what was destroyed, was what that demise yielded. Those Energies cannot be unwound, retrieved or reassembled into their "Original Wholeness" ever again.

So where does this leave *me?:* "I," left as "me," living in a "missing-octaves," "Emotional Shrapnel" reality, with the dubious endowments I inherited being Imprints, Impressions, Templates, and Stencils, all of which would be deployed in reactive style— no whole cloth, just dynamic, unconscious (to me) psychical forces that would impel me, in ignorance, on into a life full of misadventures, driven primarily by quests for the immersive oblivion of 'love,' the destructive intensity of 'hatred,' the cravings to escape what I couldn't even begin to comprehend, my addictive nature in all its multi-variegated forms, and, last but not least, a profound self-hatred that I was taught to deserve. All of these *qualities* (a term, under the circumstances, that feels like an Emotional disconnect to use in this context), gained access to the outer world by . . . . . TRIGGERING!!! . . . . . *Not* a strong hand to bring to the game of life!!

If there were one common denominator of all I have mentioned regarding my own narrative, it would be: "My life did not belong to me."

The response to my related question about "Why am I not more healed?"—at face value seeming like a kind of condemnation—a confirmation of all that I had feared without having devoted too much time probing the specifics of the question (in fear, I suppose, of the possible answer)—was a bit of a jolt. *What surprised me, however, was a sense of calm that arose within me once I was in possession of the response itself. There was something about that hard "truth," and truth, no matter what it consists of, always outranks prettied-up, shoddy, "make 'nice-nice'" content. The answer, on some level, was a confirmation of what I already knew, but I had not wanted to know it, because the truth would cost me my dream of healing, of returning to Wholeness as I (thought I) comprehended it.*

What was left for me to do was to explore the realm of Clashes of Irreconcilable Energies—and the Imprints, Impressions, Templates, Stencils and Emotional Shrapnel that grew out of these events, and explore, as best I could, how my life experience had been distended and distorted by the inheritance of smashed Wholeness, *of which the largest, damning endowment of all, was my Triggering, reactive nature.*

A flood of memories upwelled in me that dramatized the outworkings of these "endowments":

Imprints were the hard-molded scar tissue of what had happened to me.

Impressions were the indelible *Emotional* scars these imprints had left on me, which, over time, hardened into templates of reactive behaviors (Triggering).

Templates were the blueprints of my future reactive behaviors and decisions, fashioned outside of my conscious awareness.

Stencils were what I, without knowing I was doing it, projected onto others in my ongoing, present reality, through which (again unbeknownst to me), I chronically misperceived the external world, relating to it through a profoundly autonomous Triggering neurology as laced up by the traumas of long-ago which, within my unconscious being, had the Energy!!, and the fury, *as if those indignities had occurred yesterday.* Every day *"I walked through 'a forest of Triggers.'"*[34]

Emotional Shrapnel are the residues and remnants that reside in me, of all that was split asunder, expelled, propelled—ejected—outwards during the onslaught of the destruction of Inchoate Wholeness.

MORE ENCOMPASSING than just "missing octaves" in my make-up (although it includes them), Emotional Shrapnel is a kind of toxicity that runs through the marrow of every part and dimension of me—the spawn of all that was irreconcilable, which ultimately destroyed the Wholeness containing the constituent elements that would become "me." This "hangover" from "original causes and conditions" is that with which I have had to learn to coexist—the very *Energy!!* of Triggering itself—that would, much later in life, become my "partner"—the "me" vs "me" *that*

---

34. Once again I thank my Irish friend Inigo Batterham for serving up this beautiful, evocative expression.

came to fruition in, conjointly, joining forces in what would come to be called the Self-Pact.

Indeed, existing with an Imprint-driven Triggering neurology is a bit like . . . "walking around with shrapnel inside me—countless bits of sharpened iron migrating through my body, cutting my body's innards as I move—and *that happens every time I move.*"[35]

The "bottom line" (if there ever is such a thing) came to me as a Self-Pact-inspired meditation. The message was direct—factual, but not in any way accusatory or harsh:

> "Because of all that remained unknown to me over a number of decades, my endeavors, including 'falling in love' et al, driven pursuits of various career paths with earnest (conscious) intentions, seeking out levels of recognition for my gifts and talents (a way of leveraging others via manipulation to exploit them), these misplayed gifts (as in so many other areas of endeavor)—all of them amalgams of God-given talents as polluted by

---

35. Having come to recognize the profound relevance of "Emotional Shrapnel" in what formed me, both as an aftermath of "the original Clash of Irreconcilable Energies," and as such a potent factor in the phenomenon of Triggering, I wish to honor the memory of Jack Adrian, a World War II veteran who, indeed, was walking around with shrapnel in him. He was a compassionate, kind person who helped me in the early years of my sobriety. On one occasion I asked Jack more specifically about his condition. In addition to the quote (above), Jack summarized, in his laconic style, his plight as follows: "Well, Stephen, let me put it this way: For most people, World War II ended on V-J Day (15 August, 1945). For some of us, though, the war went on a while longer." A number of years following the end of the war, that migrating shrapnel within him finally took his earthly life. Jack was a living example of carrying on with life, with great dignity and poise, in the presence of an irreversible, ultimately fatal condition. I owe him.

cravings for wanton indulgence, escapism and self-aggrandizement, and compounded by the psychical cuts of gravitating Emotional Shrapnel—were not *just* destined to fail: They were '*Pre*destined to fail.' They were all attempts at 'empty-VOID-filling'—papier mâché patch-up jobs, stuffing the VOID to null out any awareness of those missing, never-to-be retrieved octaves, without which I would never be Whole."

A brief break in intensity

I KNOW THAT THIS "STUFF" that I have unloaded over this batch of pages has been pretty heavy going. Possible evidence to the contrary, I'm not really an intensity junky, nor do I aspire to be. I can't wait for this book to be completed so that I can, indeed, decouple from the intensity of its contents (believe me, I am affected by it; it takes quite a toll on me), and resume more fully my life of liberation and relative freedom in the present!

So . . . in the spirit of "coming up for a few gulps of air" before heading into the sections of Liberation and Freedom, I want to pause and, in a lighter vein, pass along some pertinent aphorisms (mostly anonymous) that have meant a lot to me, and then, at the end, include a batch of reflections which have just "shown up," from time to time, in my cranial, synaptic rodeo.

Regarding the sayings from yesteryear that were mostly gleaned from anonymous others, I really did not comprehend them at any depth when I initially heard them, but something within me impelled me to store them (awaiting later retrieval when, I would guess, I'd be more capable of understanding them). Here are ten succinct standouts for you:

(1) "You've got to get real before you get good."
(2) "You've got to feel before you can heal."
(3) "Adversity introduces us to ourselves."

(4) "The Truth will set you free, but first it will
   make you miserable."

(5) "My non-understanding has come a very long way."[36]

(6) "'Time' is God's way of not having everything happen
   all at once."

(7) "Repetition is the means for instilling unfamiliar
   truths into unwilling minds."[37]

(8) "If Justice is getting what you deserve, and Mercy
   is not getting what you deserve . . . then Grace is getting
   what you don't deserve."

(9) "You can't save face and save your ass at the same time."

(10) "When you fish in troubled waters what you catch can
   pull you in."

In addition to these stored ones, here is a group of others that
have, unbidden, arisen piecemeal in me from time to time. They
have more of a conundrum/philosophical feel to them:

(1) "When you're trying to understand yourself, you're
   trying to understand the person who's trying to understand you."

(2) "If the Universe is truly random, then 'order' is a natural
   outworking of that randomness. Otherwise, the Universe
   is not truly random."

(3) "It's important to be mindful of the distinction between
   'compassion' and 'passion.' One is noble; the other can be
   problematic."

(4) Query: "What is man, that thou art mindful of him?"
   (Psalm 8.4-d, KJB) Rejoinder: "What is it that, of

---

36. This little gem had its provenance as a spontaneous utterance by my
friend Cheryl Stevens, a former physician, now retired addictions counselor.

37. Acknowledging that this book has (by intention) numerous "repetitions"
of key themes, I hope that these perseverations may do their magic and instill
"unfamiliar truths" in helpful ways within the cranial cavities of my readers.

which to be mindful, you yourself must be?"

(5) "All truths are relative . . . including this one."

(6) "I didn't exactly 'remember' . . . Rather, I recalled that I forgot."

(7) "What you most need to know about . . . you become."

(8) "If everything is impermanent, then impermanence must also be impermanent."

(9) "If you 'feel your feelings,' but 'don't act on them' . . . they will take you to what you need to know."

(10) "It takes a pandemic to raise a book."

From Bondage to Liberation

MUCH OF WHAT I HAVE WRITTEN and reported about in this book supports my contention (spoken only about me—but *perhaps* pertaining to you as well?), that *the "cost" (maybe the "price?") of being created (at all)*—for those of us who have our root sources in Inchoate Wholeness, but for whom the actual events of being created as who we are were predicated on a shattering of that Wholeness via the Clash of Irreconcilable Emotional Energies—*has been very steep, indeed.* This has been the abiding factor, with all its negative consequences and unrecognized, latent truths within me (and maybe you, too?).

The immediate impact of these origins was to set firmly in place, before any consistent awareness had evolved, a reactive, Triggering neurology, loaded with Imprints, Impressions, Templates and their resultant Stencils, and Emotional Shrapnel, that twisted our perceptions of external reality—which came to be seen, and experienced, as a miasma of suffering, torments and provocations.

This was augmented, along the way, with conscious attempts at sustaining worthy intentions and even noble ideals—including fervent ones. But they could not be sustained when the fuel of hatred and Emotional fury would ignite into an erupting caldera, consuming our would-be goodness along with anyone and anything associated with it.

These tragic outcomes were not ones we had consciously planned, nor otherwise set out to erect. "We," with only a minimal consciousness available to us, had been repeatedly overtaken—possessed by—this poisonous spawn spewed out from our smashed Inchoate Wholeness.

The first step for achieving any sort of liberation from such a heartless, imposing tyranny was recognizing its existence within us. As I have been at pains to present throughout this book, becoming conscious of being so ruled by such painful, brutish forces could be gained only by holding them, in full potency, *without unleashing them*—a near impossible task. What paved the way to make this at all possible was the birth of enough *conscience*, which could begin to register the consequences of all the destructiveness that seemed to flow through, and from, us like a curse. And ... *this* recognition could *only* transpire if we were in such an extreme level of torment that the "we" in each of us—our ego consciousness and the Energies of Triggering—became willing to "cut a deal" to go to any lengths to STOP THE DESTRUCTION!!!!

Escapist, craving-driven behaviors, the pervasive stock-in-trade leading up to the aforementioned dilemma, became—as we commenced to reckon with some of the more obvious ones: alcoholism, drug addiction, sex and 'love' addiction, urge-to-power addiction, quite possibly anger and rage addiction, compulsive overeating/eating "disorders," etc. (along with our own personal additional repertoire of escapist behaviors and unruly Emotions)—pathways to discover, within our now clearer vision, that our reactive, Triggering destructiveness *was still there*, parading and masquerading around in *other* guises, which, minus the indulgences we had previously been involved with, were taking on a hue of legitimacy and acceptability, *giving* evidence of being a dodge—a kind of behavioral camouflage—a "cover up"—of what was still transpiring, in all its ugliness, just beneath the surface.

And . . . all this time, with whatever awarenesses we possessed, we thought that "we" were electively doing it all—choosing it as an exercise of our presumed (though fictitious) righteously-come-by "free will"—not knowing that the forces of Emotional Torments and Emotional Shrapnel, incessantly operating and influencing us behind the scenes, were autonomous, and "we" were their victims.

Out of the consequences which resulted from this mishegaas came, finally, the Self-Pact—resorted to, from a state of desperation, as the "last house on the block"—a last chance, beyond which only final tragedy and perdition awaited.

There was no guarantee that such an approach stood any real chance of working as an honest, deep-reaching method of encountering our "masters" (whom we didn't even know existed), let alone reaching a point of working *with* the Energies of Triggering which were both their presence and their language. But, past attempts at remediation via other approaches had proved wanting, and there was nothing else to try.

With the immediate Self-Pact goal of, by and large, ceasing to unleash "our" destructive behavior onto others in the external world, and, to cease, as best we could, making wholesale misattributions to these others as to "their provocations"—and therefore, *their* being responsible for our unleashings on them—we welcomed this progress and, as Triggering was structural to our makeup and, therefore, ongoing (as expected), we continued to default instantly to the Self-Pact whenever Triggering would occur.

We were becoming more and more practiced at "riding the Energies inwards," and seeing what *"their"* agenda was. Indeed, we discovered that the Energies' objective—now given a chance, with our attentive consciousness following it—was to share "their" (and our) story with us—was, in the fullness of time, to revert to—to direct our attention to—the original causes and conditions of our origins, from Inchoate Wholeness through the Clash of Irreconcilable Emotional Energies—all part of the original causes and conditions that created "us"—*not* as "whole people," *but as fractured shards, splinters and riven with Emotional Shrapnel, with the "deck stacked against us"*—as people who, left to our own devices, would *always*, through cravings and escapist behaviors and indulgences of all sorts, be prone to seeking even a hint of an immersion that could, however momentarily, appear to recreate a "Wholeness" moment—to stuff the "VOID" with *something.* Many of us, previously, had found an ephemeral payoff of this sort in our pursuit of "oblivion" experiences.

And so . . . as our march towards personal liberation from the tyranny of "original causes and conditions" and their spawn: Imprints, Impressions, Templates, Stencils and Emotional Shrapnel has continued; as we have gained proficiency in recognizing our reactive, Triggering neurology, along with our heretofore unconscious projections—the misattributions of "provocations" onto the outer world; as we have come to recognize our distended ways of perceiving and experiencing what we took to be the "outer world"—the supposed "justifications" of all our unleashings; as we have continued to become increasingly aware of *all* of the above, *as revealed to us by the actual Triggered Energies themselves* (now, with mutual benefit, well-harnessed by the Self-Pact)— *WE were well on the road to liberation from all of that bondage!!*

It was time for a hijacked life to be, *finally,* turned over to its rightful owner. If not in the form of some sort of restored, original, or Inchoate, "Wholeness," then, at least, in the form of a true liberation from the stranglehold that had resulted from that potential Wholeness's having been destroyed. *Liberation could still be ours.*

On to Freedom

As a former friend of mine (now deceased) used to say, by way of admonition, "'Awakening' is just the first moments of being awake."[38]

---

38. This simple-sounding but *very* astute observation was made by Daniel

And so it is.

It may seem a bit odd to refer to "liberation" and "freedom" within the context of continuing to coexist with forces that still have it, within *their* power, to be devastatingly destructive. Instincts are like that, and most people, I feel obliged to say, are feeling their way along knife-edge ridges without their being aware of it.

I, for one, *am* aware of it, and that makes the precipitous trail, with its sharp drop-offs on either side, very real to me. Prior to becoming aware of this I lived, in defiant ignorance, as a thumb-my-nose daredevil, oblivious to the perilous world and the risks I was taking. The peril did not depend upon my awareness, or lack thereof, to be real. *It had always been there.*

What I lacked in all those years, and decades, was having anything resembling "informed choice" on things I *thought* "I" was deciding to set out to do—all the while in ignorance of any possible deeper self-understanding, and *always* in a thoroughly self-centered, exploitive, indulgent manner.

Over these past 11-plus years, The Self-Pact helped me to save my marriage—but it could not remedy my Triggering neurology. That I was, and am, stuck with. But . . . the *Energy!*, as has been painstakingly reported, turned out to be capable of filling pedagogical—even, at times, psychopomp-like, roles. As I followed the Energy inwards via the Self-Pact, in sync with Triggering's ongoing daily occurrences, it led me deeper and deeper into my (dare I say: DEEP!)—even pre-verbal and pre-memory (as memory is construed nowadays)—past.

Determined to have a life, to live fully and lovingly despite *knowingly* having to coexist with that which could destroy us, led us—when the conditions were ripe for it, and we had become

---

Hobbing, an All-Harvard Scholar, 45 years ago. Our friendship did not last (nor, lamentably, did his life), but his brilliant quip has always stayed with me, "going the distance."

willing to "go to any lengths" not to lay waste to everything—to the Self-Pact, which, in turn, created within us a cooperative arrangement between "us"—*including the forces of Emotional violence.*

Having a life grounded on this basis builds on itself, and comes to be a profound awakening, and realization, for us, that we are living in a state of freedom. We have arrived at a blessed state of being that had so long eluded us. Now it is ours, with which to live as wonderfully transformed a life as we can. New adventures surely await us.

Intimations of a (possible) Wholeness (?)

A QUESTION HAS OCCURRED TO ME in the whole process of encountering, immersively, my origins within "Inchoate Wholeness." I have no answer to this question but I might as well pose it:

Is it possible that even "Inchoate Wholeness" grows tired of its own "sameness" of being whole? Going back again to the Big Bang 13.7 billion years ago, was there a complete, whole universe that had preceded the Big Bang?—perhaps a universe that had run its own gamut from "original creation" through its own "life"—evolutionary—epochs, accomplishing, over billions of years (of however in that previous universe the dimension of "time" was construed and tallied), and achieving, "final" integrative Wholeness at some point—which then became a stasis, which then became celestially "boring" (however *that* might have been perceived), leading to a "Divine" dissatisfaction with all that had seemed "completed?"

Was it "time," within the thought structure of—the consciousness within—that previous universe, to "reshuffle the deck"—to play, on a trans-cosmic scale, "52 Card Pickup?"—to shatter its own Wholeness, giving way to spawn a new universe: the one that, having created us, is now *our* abode? **Im**ploding in previous dimensions = **Ex**ploding in newly created dimensions?

If there is even a grain of possible truth to this, relative to our *own, personal, ephemeral lifespan in this Universe, do we—who are, possibly, just fragments and shards—Emotional Shrapnel—of a preceding "Inchoate Wholeness"—carry to any extent the Resonance— the Energy—not just of that primordial cataclysm, but also that inherent "Wholeness" that **preceded** it? Is **that** "Wholeness" something not to be returned to, but, rather, something to be **reinvented anew**?*

And . . . *if* our Universe, including every little jot and tittle of it, is a projection of an "implicate order"—a hologram—so the theory goes, then every scintilla of creation is encoded there, *and . . . each one of us contains within us **some** amount, even if it's only a subatomic "millimicron," of the "DNA" of Wholeness—the "BIG PICTURE"—along with how to awaken and activate it.*

In the "VOID" we feel, in our ignorance, the absence of a craving-based wholeness within our own lives. Within, all around, and through, the misplaced strivings (cravings) for power, prestige, romance, influence, stature, lust and passion that constitute so much of our perfunctory, prosaic (often duplicit) "practice" of "morality," "ethics," "conscience," and even "religion"—as we try to "stuff the VOID" with *"something!"*—these very qualities, *when fully and actively encountered **on their own terms** via the Self-Pact,* take up the opportunity, and ability, to guide us in ways in which we may indeed become capable of living out, and bequeathing, a contribution of *our own searching,* soul and substance in furtherance of a *new awakening*—perhaps "the very first moments of being awake"—of an as-yet-to-be-fully-realized resilient manifestation of a New Wholeness . . . maybe even one in which the VOID itself is not an absence of that which we crave and have lost, but (just maybe) a repository—maybe even a source—of a phenomenon of Wholeness that human consciousness has yet to experience, and make its own.

*Is it too much to wish that maybe . . . just maybe . . . in the fullness of time and existence, "the Clash of Irreconcilable Emotions" transforms, somehow—to be recast as "the Reunion of chastened, **now reconcilable properties of Emotional Wholeness**—no longer merely "inchoate," but*

"CHOATE!!"—not just "potential," but **established, actual and real, as experienced through the very VOID that we fear?**

For those of us who have made it through the torments, have established our liberation, and now have "freedom to live," this possible calling to a new level of Wholeness beckons us onwards. Our hard-earned, exuberantly lived-out freedom, exacted at such heavy cost, has now become a buoyant, celebratory participation in an unfolding joy.

Help light the way if you can.
Yours, very truly, with the love of a kindred spirit,

—Stephen Rich Merriman

Afterword

THANK YOU, MY DEAR READERS, for coursing through this book, and possibly others that I have written.

My intention has been to write books that I wish had been there to help me, at an earlier stage of life, had someone else already written them, and, that being the case, had I stumbled upon them. I hope my efforts have stirred you in fruitful directions—the exact experience that I have had in the process of writing them!

I have, more or less, retired, having survived, over many years and decades, four careers along the way —jazz pianist/composer, psychotherapist, corporate consultant (critical incident stress debriefings/interventions), and author of a number of nonfiction books. The "authoring," "jazz pianist/composer" activities, along with occasional teaching roles in my areas of alleged expertise, are continuing, much to my delight (and at a more relaxed pace), on into my "senior-hood." My learning how to be a devoted, capable-of-loving husband and father to a much younger family, and an equally loving and available father and grandfather to my grown children, and their children, has taught me more about how to be human—more loving, less selfish. It is here, within my family (both immediate and extended), that my happiness is most rooted, and resides. Occasionally, at my age, I notice that the "park benches" are starting to look kind of good to me . . . but I cannot yet, at this point, afford to sit down on them and go mesmerizingly vacant. There's just so much that is still going on, for which my whole-hearted participation is needed, solicited . . . and, wonder of wonders, valued.

Having been a city kid most of my life, I now appreciate living in a sub-rural region of Western Massachusetts, with a magnificent view of the Connecticut River Valley just minutes from our home. I do experience myself as being relatively at peace—as an "elder"(junior-grade) of sorts—reaping what I have sown, both "+" and "-" over previous years and decades (and lifetimes?). The harder lessons, thoroughly deserved, seem pretty well digested at this point, and I pray that they stay that way. The gentler, more blissful harvestings are here now, with greater frequency, and I accept them (as I learn to trust them more) as gracefully and gratefully as I can.

A former client of mine (during my psychotherapist years) had a kind of benediction she liked to say at the end of each of our clinical sessions. I send it along to you, on her behalf:

"Many blessings to you on your sacred journey."

—S.R.M.

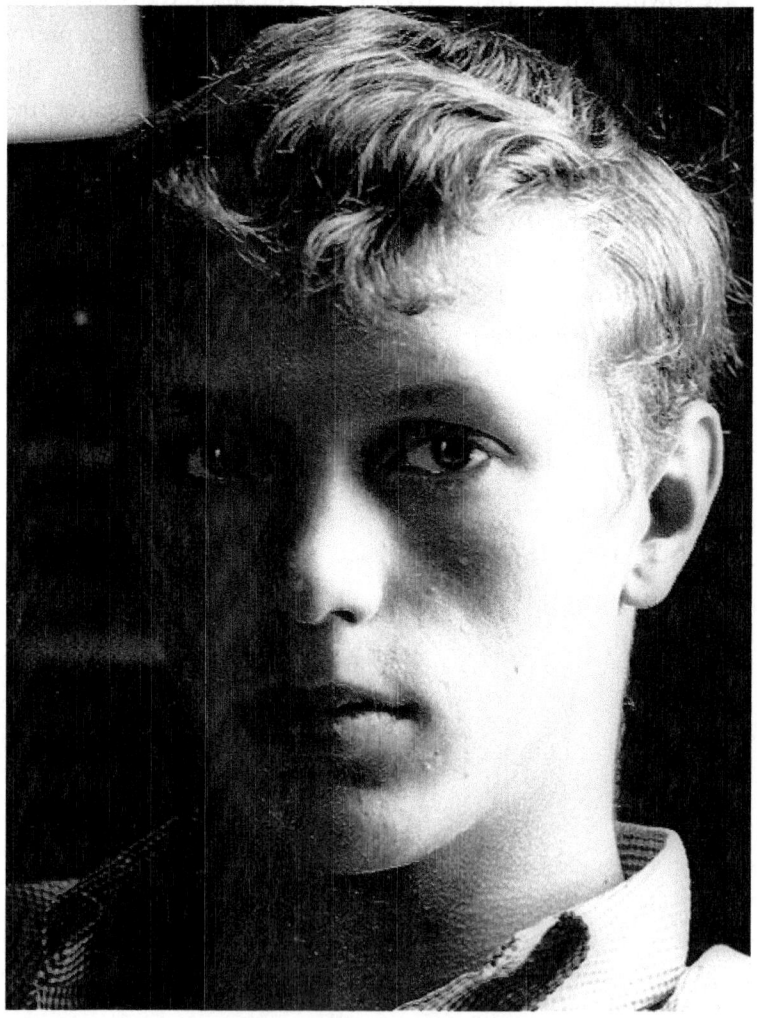

Age 18—desperate, hungry, fraught, lost, and danger-ridden [41]

---

41. Thanks go out to my teenage chum Mark Solomon for taking this deeply personal photograph of "me" in 1965, and then, unbidden, 49 years later, sending this image along to me. Many blessings to you, Mark.

Age 74—a bit more "chill" (Thank you, dearest Emily, for taking this photograph of me.)

NOTES

NOTES

Printed by BoD™in Norderstedt, Germany

9 780981 769882